THINK LIKE A GENIUS

44 Mind-Blowing Questions & Answers
for Curious Kids — Explore Science,
Space, Nature, and Inventions

Table of contents

How do airplanes stay in the air? 10

What's the secret behind robots that can think? 14

How do 3D printers work, and what can they make?
.... 18

Why don't we feel the Earth spinning? 22

What is a black hole, and why is it so powerful? 26

How do video games get made? 30

How do self-driving cars know where to go? 36

Who invented the light bulb? 42

How do people come up with world-changing ideas?
.... 46

What's the most famous invention made by accident?
.... 50

Can kids invent things too? 54

Activity Idea: Invent Your Own Thing! 58

What is biomimicry, and how can nature inspire inventions? 62

How do stars and planets form? 70

How do astronauts sleep in space? 74

Why doesn't the sun burn out? 78

Can we live on Mars one day? 82

How do astronauts go to the bathroom in space? ... 86

Why do astronauts need spacesuits? 90

How do jellyfish glow in the dark? 96

What's the strongest animal on Earth? 100

Why do birds fly south for the winter? 104

What's the fastest creature on land? 108

What's on the inside of a turtle's shell? 112

Can plants talk to each other? 116

Why do bees use hexagons to build their hives? 120

Why is my snot yellow when I'm sick? 126

How do muscles grow when we exercise? 130

Why do we get goosebumps? 134

What makes our heart beat faster when we're scared?
.... 138

Why do we dream when we sleep? 142

How do vaccines help us stay healthy? 146

How many colors can the human eye see? 152

Why do fireflies light up? 156

Why do some animals never need to drink water?
.... 160

Why do onions make us cry? 164

How old is the oldest living tree? 168

Who was Leonardo da Vinci, and why was he a genius?
.... 174

Who is Albert Einstein, and why is he considered one of
the smartest people ever? 178

Who is Ada Lovelace, and why is she called the first
computer programmer? 182

Who was Marie Curie, and how did she change science
forever? 186

Who built Stonehenge, and why? 192

What's really going on in the Bermuda Triangle? .. 196

What's at the bottom of the ocean? 200

Time to Think Like a Genius! 204

Glossary 208

Back Blurb 214

Alright, time to level up with facts you didn't even know you needed! Ever think about how planes just stay in the sky, or how robots can straight-up think like humans? Well, you've just unlocked the ultimate guide to mind-blowing stuff that's gonna have you saying, *'Wait, how did I not know that?!'*

This book's like your *VIP pass* to the coolest mysteries out there — science, space, nature, inventions, and even the super-weird facts that'll have your brain doing backflips. We're diving into the wildest questions, like why the Earth doesn't feel like a spinny ride (even though it's zooming fast), how video games come to life, and what would happen if you fell into a black hole (spoiler: *it's CRAZY*).

And we're not stopping there! Ever wonder why bees are all about hexagons or how astronauts catch some Z's while floating around in space? We've got you! By the time you're done, you'll be flexing all your genius-level knowledge and impressing everyone around you.

So, you ready to blast off into a world of epic questions and even more epic answers? Grab your thinking cap (and some snacks, obviously), because we're about to dive into some seriously cool stuff together!

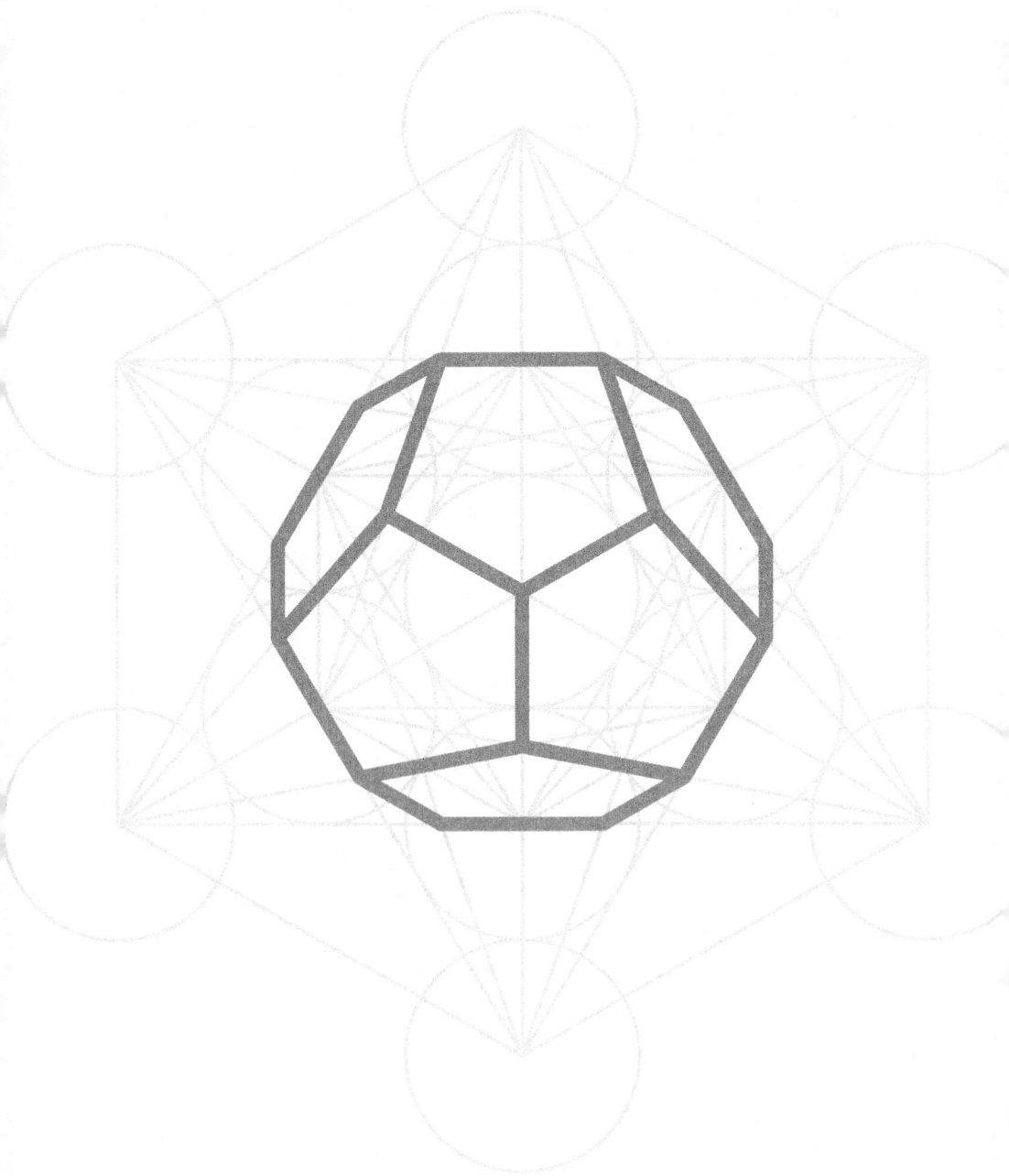

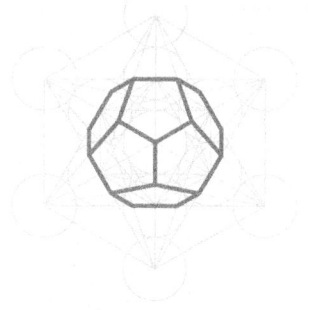

SCIENCE & TECHNOLOGY

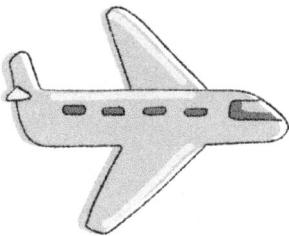

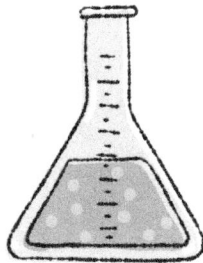

HOW DO AIRPLANES STAY IN THE AIR?

Alright, picture this: a plane flies by juggling four forces like a pro – lift, thrust, drag, and gravity – all working together to keep it cruising in the sky!

✳ **Lift:** This is the plane's superpower! The wings are shaped in a way that makes air zoom faster on top and slower underneath, kinda like magic. This creates a push from below that keeps the plane floating up like a boss.

✳ **Thrust:** The plane's engines (think *turbo boosters*) give it that vroom forward, helping it zoom through the air. Thrust is like the energy drink that powers the whole thing.

* **Drag:** But hold up, not everything's smooth sailing. There's air trying to slow the plane down – that's drag. It's like the air saying, "Woah, slow your roll!" But the plane's sleek design keeps it dodging drag like a ninja.

* **Gravity:** Now, gravity's that friend who keeps pulling the plane down to Earth, like, *"Come back!"* But the plane just flexes its wings and engines, saying, *"Nah, I'm staying up here!"*

So, when these forces are in check – lift beats gravity, and thrust outruns drag – the plane's flying high, cruising through the sky like a total legend!

FUN FACT: Did you know that the fastest passenger plane ever was the Concorde, and it could fly faster than the speed of sound? That means it could travel from New York to London in just about 3.5 hours! Most planes today take 7-8 hours to make that trip.

WHAT'S THE SECRET BEHIND ROBOTS THAT CAN THINK?

Ever wonder how robots seem so smart, like they stepped out of a sci-fi movie? Spoiler alert: it's not magic, it's something called *Artificial Intelligence, or AI*. And AI is basically the robot's brain that lets them do way more than just follow commands.

Think about teaching a robot to play soccer. At first, it'll totally miss the ball, but the more it practices, the better it gets. This is called machine learning. It's just like you playing a game — at first, you might be bad, but the more you play, the more you crush it!

Robots don't have regular eyes or ears like we do, but they've got their own version: sensors! Sensors help robots "see" and "hear" what's going on around them. So if a robot is about to run into a wall, its sensors give it a heads-up, and it stops — kinda like how you dodge a ball flying at your face.

But how do robots know what to do? They follow algorithms, which are like cheat codes or recipes that tell them how to react. For example, if a robot spots a ball rolling toward it, the algorithm decides: kick it or dodge it. Easy, right?

Some robots even have neural networks, which are like mini robot brains that help them figure out patterns. This means they can tell the difference between, say, a human and a tree. It's kinda like how your phone recognizes your face to unlock itself — robots use the same brainpower to understand their world better.

$$Hp_{(m)} =$$

$$C = 2 \times 0.5 \times \frac{22}{7} = \frac{22}{7}$$

So, next time you see a robot doing something super smart, it's all thanks to AI, sensors, and algorithms working together. Robots are learning new stuff every day, just like you! How cool is that?

HOW DO 3D PRINTERS WORK, AND WHAT CAN THEY MAKE?

Imagine if you could build anything you wanted layer by layer, like stacking *LEGO* bricks but way cooler. That's basically what a 3D printer does!

Here's how it works: First, you design something on a computer, like a toy, a tool, or even a whole building! The 3D printer then reads that design and starts "printing" it out in real life. But instead of using ink like a normal printer, it uses plastic, metal, or other materials. It melts the material and builds your design layer by layer until — **boom!** — you've got a real-life object.

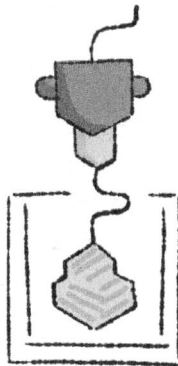

It's a bit like frosting a cake, but each layer of frosting is melted material that hardens into your final design.

The printer keeps stacking those layers on top of each other until the object is done.

So, what can 3D printers make? The possibilities are endless! People use 3D printers to create toys, custom phone cases, tools, and even food — yep, there are 3D printers that can "print" pizza! Scientists and engineers are using them to make everything from tiny parts for rockets to life-sized houses, and even body parts like bones or organs!

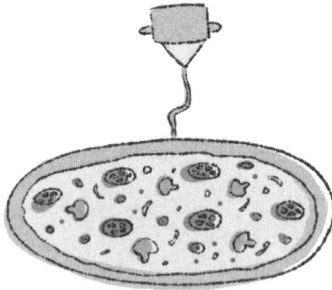

Pretty awesome, right? With a 3D printer, you can turn almost any idea into a real thing.

WHY DON'T WE FEEL THE EARTH SPINNING?

It's wild to think that the Earth is spinning at about 1,000 miles per hour at the equator! But here's the big question: why don't we feel like we're on a giant merry-go-round?

Let's break it down. First, Earth is massive — way bigger than we can really imagine — so it spins super smoothly. Everything on Earth, including you, me, and everything we see, is moving along with it at the same speed. It's like when you're in a car driving down the highway. As long as the ride is smooth, you don't feel like you're going fast, even though the car is speeding down the road. You can talk, play games, and even eat snacks without noticing the speed. Same with Earth — because everything is moving at the same speed (the air, land, us!), it feels like we're standing still.

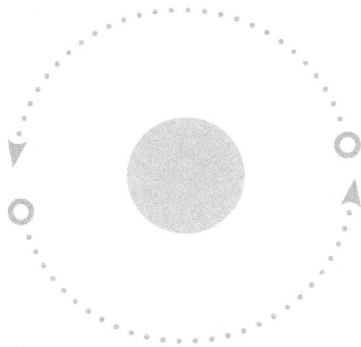

The Earth also spins really evenly, without any big bumps or jerks. If it suddenly stopped or sped up, we'd definitely feel that, like if a car slammed on the brakes. But since the spin is steady, we don't feel any changes.

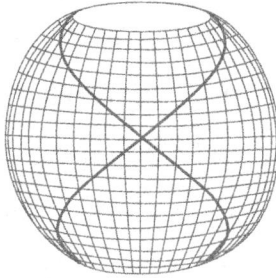

Then there's *gravity*, which is like Earth's invisible seatbelt. Gravity is pulling everything towards the center of the Earth, holding us down, so even though the Earth is spinning fast, gravity keeps us from flying off into space!

FUN FACT: The speed of Earth's spin depends on where you are! If you're standing at the equator, you're moving the fastest — over 1,000 miles per hour. But if you're at the North or South Pole, you're barely moving at all, because you're at the center of the spin! It's like the middle of a record player — it spins the slowest at the center and the fastest at the edge.

WHAT IS A BLACK HOLE, AND WHY IS IT SO POWERFUL?

A black hole is one of the craziest and most powerful things in space! Imagine a giant vacuum cleaner that can suck in everything around it — even light! That's right, a black hole is so powerful that not even light can escape once it gets too close.

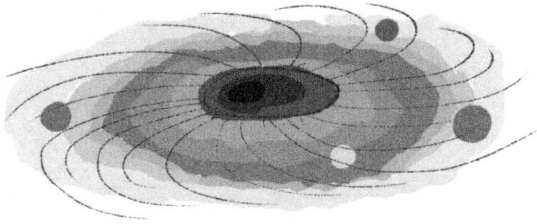

Here's how it works: a black hole forms when a massive star reaches the end of its life and collapses in on itself. All the star's mass gets squished into a super tiny space called a singularity, where gravity becomes incredibly strong. This gravity is so powerful that it pulls in everything nearby — planets, stars, light, and anything else that dares to get too close. Once something crosses a point called the event horizon (the black hole's *"point of no return"*), it's gone forever!

The reason black holes are so powerful is because of their insane gravity. The more mass something has, the stronger its gravity. Since all the mass of a star is packed into such a tiny space, black holes have extreme gravity, making them the ultimate space traps!

FUN FACT: If you got close to a black hole (which I don't recommend!), time would slow down for you compared to someone far away. This is called time dilation. Near the black hole's massive gravity, time stretches out, so if you could somehow survive near a black hole, you'd see the universe speeding up around you while you're moving in super slow-mo!

HOW DO VIDEO GAMES GET MADE?

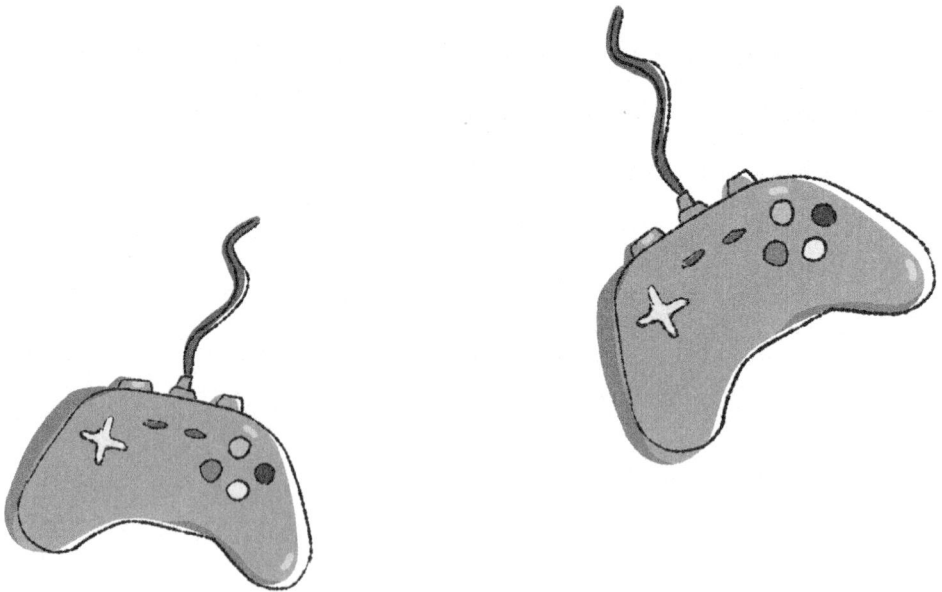

Ever wondered how your favorite video games come to life, packed with cool characters, awesome levels, and mind-blowing graphics? Making a video game is like building a whole digital universe from scratch, and it takes a ton of creativity and teamwork to make it happen. Let's break it down!

Step 1: The Big Idea

It all starts with a cool idea! Game developers think up the story, characters, and gameplay. They decide if it'll be a racing game, adventure, or puzzle. Once the plan is ready, they write a script that lays out the story, levels, and goals—just like a movie.

Step 2: Designing the World

Then, the designers jump in. They create everything you see in the game, from characters to backgrounds. Whether it's a real-life city or a fantasy world, designers make sure the game looks awesome, whether cartoonish or super realistic!

Step 3: The Coding Magic

Now comes the real magic — *coding*! This is where the programmers come in and make everything work. Think of coding as the language that tells the computer or console what to do. Without coding, your character wouldn't even move!

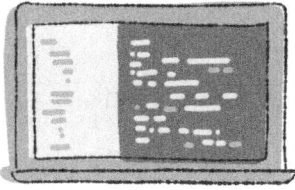

Most games are built using a game engine like *Unity* or *Unreal Engine*. These engines are like giant toolboxes filled with coding tools. Programmers write code in special languages like *C++*, *Python*, or *C#* to create all the actions you see in the game. For example, they'll write code that says, *"When the player presses the spacebar, make the character jump,"* or *"If the character bumps into a wall, stop moving."*

Coding also handles physics (like how fast things move or fall) and *AI (Artificial Intelligence)*, which controls how smart the game's enemies or non-player characters (NPCs) act. That's how your enemies know when to attack or how to hide from you!

GAME OVER

Programmers also write code to handle the game's graphics and animations — making sure the characters move smoothly, the scenery changes, and even how the light and shadows look. And don't forget about the sound effects! Coders make sure the right sounds play at the right time, like when you pick up an item or a door creaks open in a spooky game.

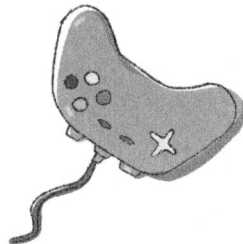

Step 4: Testing and Fixing

Once the coding is done, it's time for the testers to jump in. Their job is to play the game over and over, finding bugs (or glitches) in the code. If something in the game doesn't work right — like a character getting stuck in a wall — he testers report it, and the programmers fix it. This process is called *debugging* and can take a while, but it's super important to make sure the game runs smoothly.

Step 5: Release and Updates

When the game is finally ready and all the bugs are fixed, it gets released for players like you to enjoy! But even after a game is out, developers often keep improving it with updates, adding new levels, characters, or features to keep players hooked.

So the next time you play a video game, remember that behind every character, jump, and epic boss fight, there's a whole team of people bringing that digital world to life!

FUN FACT: Games often use scripts, which are short bursts of code that make things happen at specific times, like triggering a boss battle or starting a cutscene. It's like having a set of instructions ready to go when certain conditions are met.

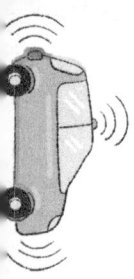

HOW DO SELF-DRIVING CARS KNOW WHERE TO GO?

Self-driving cars are like futuristic robots that navigate the roads all on their own! They use sensors, cameras, and radar to gather tons of information about what's happening around them— like other cars, pedestrians, and road signs. These tools help the car "see" its surroundings, and the data gets processed super fast.

But here's where the real magic happens: *Artificial Intelligence (AI)!* The car's AI is like its brain, analyzing all the information from the sensors and making decisions in real time. It tells the car when to stop at a red light, turn left or right, or even slow down if something suddenly jumps into the road. AI uses maps and GPS to know where the car is, figure out the best route, and keep it on track. It's like the world's smartest GPS!

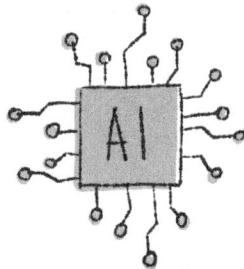

The coolest part? These cars actually learn from experience using machine learning. Just like how you get better at riding a bike or playing a video game the more you practice, self-driving cars get better at driving the more they're on the road. They "remember" tricky situations they've encountered, like sharp turns or heavy traffic, and improve for next time.

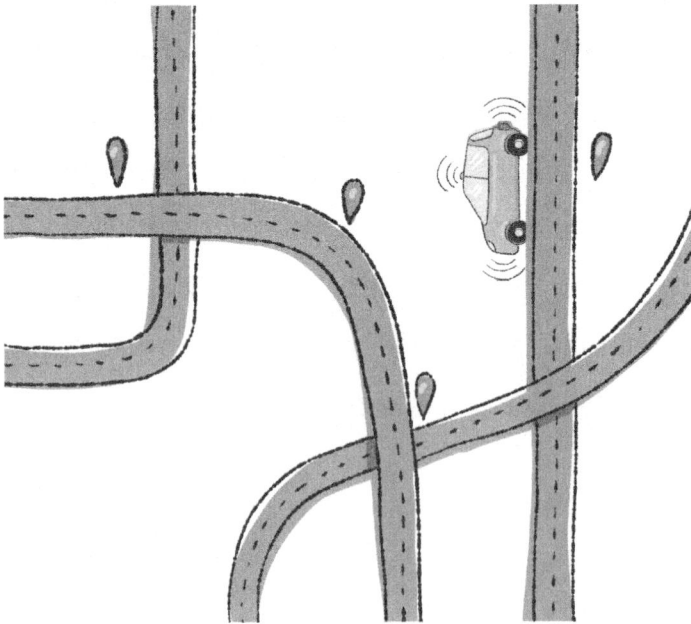

FUN FACT: Self-driving cars also have something called LiDAR, which uses lasers to map out the environment in 3D! It's like giving the car superpowers to detect objects even in tough conditions like rain or fog.

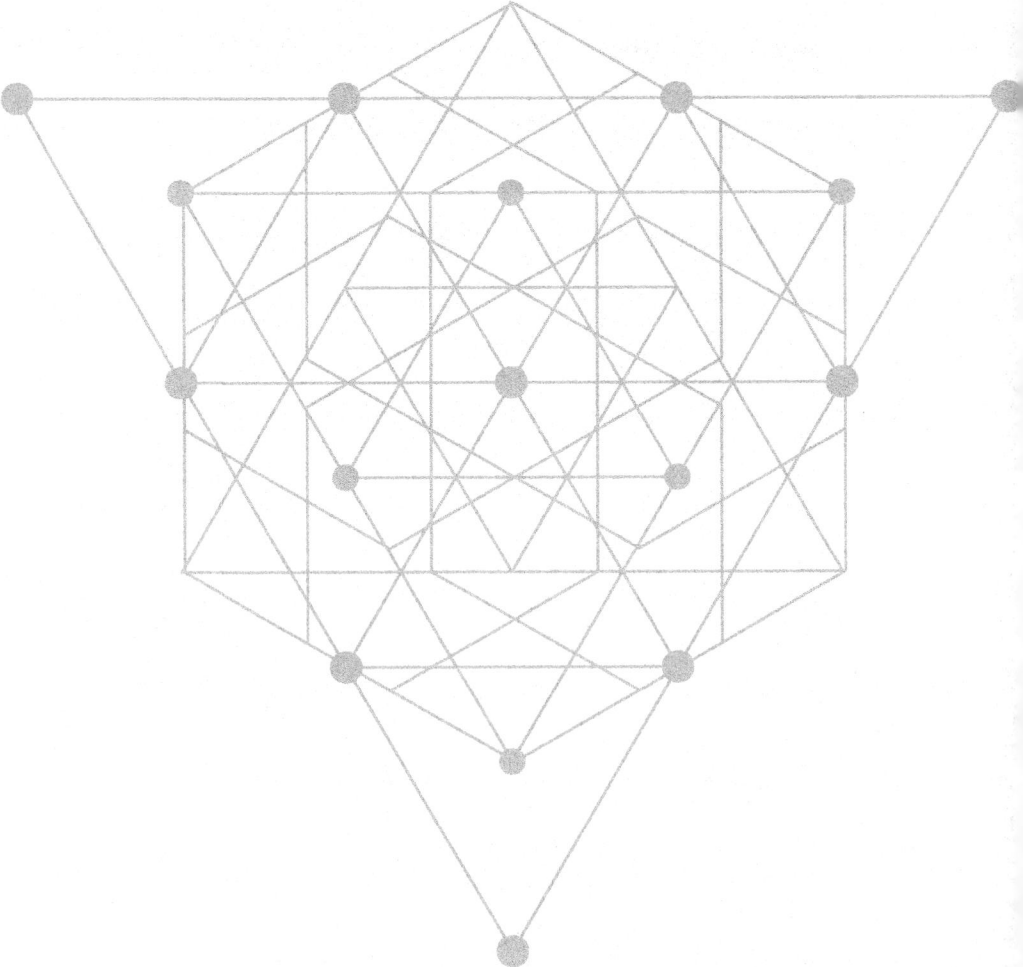

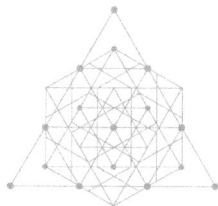

INVENTIONS & CREATIVITY

WHO INVENTED THE LIGHT BULB?

Most people say *Thomas Edison* invented the light bulb, but the story's a bit more complicated! While Edison made the first long-lasting, practical light bulb in 1879, he wasn't the only one working on it. In fact, many inventors before him tried to create light bulbs, but their versions didn't last very long or were too expensive.

Edison's big breakthrough was finding the right material for the filament (the part that glows). He used carbonized bamboo, which made the bulb last much longer than earlier designs. He also developed a system to deliver electricity to homes, which made his light bulb even more useful.

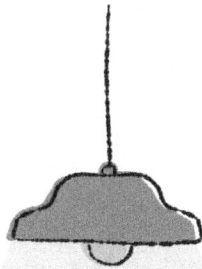

But let's not forget *Sir Humphry Davy*, who created the first electric light way back in 1802, and *Joseph Swan*, a British inventor who made his own working light bulb around the same time as Edison. In fact, Swan and Edison eventually teamed up and shared credit for the invention!

FUN FACT: Edison's light bulbs could stay lit for over 1,200 hours, which was a huge deal back then! Before light bulbs, people had to rely on candles and gas lamps to light their homes.

HOW DO PEOPLE COME UP WITH WORLD-CHANGING IDEAS?

The secret to coming up with game-changing ideas? Think BIG, just like *Elon Musk!* He's the mastermind behind some of the coolest projects on the planet — and beyond. Instead of sticking to the regular stuff, he's always asking, "What's the next impossible thing we can make possible?"

Let's take a look at his projects: with *Tesla,* he didn't just want to build cool electric cars, he wanted to change the entire car industry and help save the planet from pollution. He's like, "*Why rely on gas when we can power cars with clean energy?*" Now, Teslas are some of the fastest and smartest cars out there, proving that electric cars can be fun, fast, and eco-friendly.

Then there's *SpaceX* — Musk didn't just want to explore space, he wanted to make it so anyone could eventually travel to other planets! He started asking crazy questions like, "*Why are rockets so expensive? What if we*

could use them over and over again like planes?" After a few epic explosions (oops), SpaceX became the first company to land reusable rockets, and now he's setting his sights on Mars! Yep, Musk wants to build a colony on the red planet.

But that's not all — he's also working on *Neuralink*, a project that aims to connect our brains to computers. It sounds like something out of a sci-fi movie, but Musk thinks it could help people with brain injuries or even let us talk to computers with our minds. How wild is that?

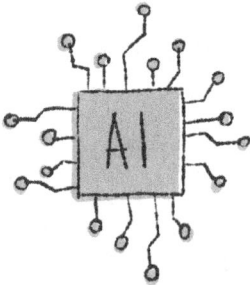

So how does he dream up these crazy ideas? One of Musk's tricks is called first principles thinking. Basically, he breaks down a problem to its most basic parts, then rebuilds the solution from scratch. Like with SpaceX, instead of just tweaking existing rockets, he asked, *"What are rockets made of, and can we build them cheaper?"* That's how he figured out

how to make reusable rockets.

Musk is also always learning. He's constantly reading, studying new subjects like physics and AI, and surrounding himself with experts who help turn his bold ideas into reality. He's not afraid to fail either— he knows that every failure teaches him something new, getting him one step closer to success.

So whether it's revolutionizing cars, exploring space, or connecting brains to computers, Elon Musk's projects show that when you dream big, keep learning, and take risks, you can come up with ideas that could literally change the world!

WHAT'S THE MOST FAMOUS INVENTION MADE BY ACCIDENT?

Some of the coolest inventions in history were total accidents! One of the most famous? *Penicillin* — the world's first antibiotic that's saved millions of lives. It all started when a scientist named *Alexander Fleming* left some petri dishes out while he went on vacation (yep, a real vacation!). When he came back, he noticed mold growing on one of the dishes, but something weird was happening — the bacteria around the mold had died. That mold turned out to be *Penicillium*, and it was the key to creating antibiotics, which we now use to fight infections.

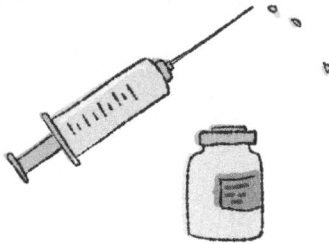

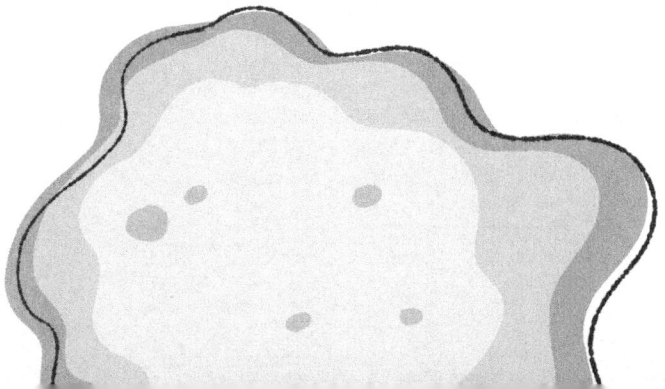

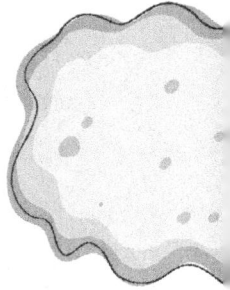

Another famous accidental invention is *Sticky Notes*. A scientist named Spencer Silver was actually trying to make a super-strong glue, but he accidentally created a super-weak one instead. His sticky-but-removable adhesive didn't seem useful at first — until his colleague, *Art Fry*, had the genius idea to use it for bookmarks that wouldn't fall out of his choir book. **Boom** — *Sticky Notes* were born, and now they're everywhere!

FUN FACT: Even chocolate chip cookies were invented by accident! Ruth Wakefield was trying to make chocolate cookies but ran out of baker's chocolate, so she threw in chunks of regular chocolate, thinking they'd melt. Spoiler: they didn't, and the chocolate chip cookie was born!

Turns out, sometimes accidents lead to the tastiest (or most lifesaving) inventions!

CAN KIDS INVENT THINGS TOO?

Totally! Kids have some of the most creative minds out there, and they've come up with ideas that have straight-up changed the game. Some of the coolest stuff we use today was invented by kids just like you!

Take *Chester Greenwood*, for example. When he was 15, he was tired of freezing his ears off while ice skating, so he whipped up a pair of earmuffs. He took some fur, stuck it on a wire, and boom—no more frosty ears. And guess what? People still rock earmuffs today! Pretty legendary, right?

Then there's *Alayna G.*, who was only 8 when she came up with a solar-powered car seat cooler. She was tired of getting roasted by hot car seats in the summer and thought, "Why not use the sun to cool them down?" Now that's a next-level hack!

And let's not forget *Gitanjali Rao*. At just 11, she invented a device to detect lead in drinking water after hearing about the water crisis in Flint, Michigan. Her invention? Straight-up genius — it could help millions of people get safe drinking water.

ACTIVITY IDEA: INVENT YOUR OWN THING!

Alright, now it's your turn to flex those brain muscles and get creative! Here's a fun challenge to level up your inner inventor:

1. **Spot a Problem**: Take a look around — whether it's at home, school, or anywhere you hang out. What's something that bugs you or could be way better? Maybe it's *tangled headphones, a messy desk,* or even *shoes* that come untied too easily. Whatever it is, find your problem.

2. **Brainstorm Fixes**: Now think about how you can fix it. Don't hold back — even the craziest ideas can lead to something epic. Think about solutions that no one else has come up with yet.

3. **Sketch It Out**: Grab some paper and sketch your invention. Add all the cool details — what it looks like, how it works, and what makes it awesome. Give it a catchy name, too — because every great invention needs one!

4. **Make a Prototype**: If you can, try to create a mini version using stuff around the house like cardboard, tape, or even *LEGOs*. It doesn't have to be perfect — it's just a test run to show off your idea.

5. **Show It Off**: Share your invention with friends or family and explain how it works. Who knows — you might have the next big thing on your hands!

FUN FACT: There are legit kid inventor contests out there, like the Google Science Fair and the Young Inventors Challenge, where you can submit your ideas and maybe even turn them into real products. So, go wild with your ideas — kids can totally invent stuff that changes the world!

Ready to invent? Let's go!

WHAT IS BIOMIMICRY, AND HOW CAN NATURE INSPIRE INVENTIONS?

Ever think about how nature totally nails solving problems? That's where biomimicry comes in — it's like humans copying the life hacks from plants, animals, and ecosystems to create inventions that are next-level. Basically, inventors and scientists are out here taking notes from nature's genius designs to make stuff that works better and smarter.

CHECK THIS OUT: say someone's trying to make something that's super strong but still light. Instead of making it up, they can just look at how spiders spin their webs. Did you know *spider silk* is stronger than *steel* but crazy light? By studying that, we've invented new materials that are just as strong and flexible. Nature's low-key been engineering for millions of years, so why not borrow a trick or two?

Here are some epic examples of biomimicry in action:

Velcro: Ever had those annoying burrs stick to your socks when you're outside? Turns out, that's where *Velcro* came from! A scientist, *George de Mestral,* peeped how burrs clung to fabric and thought (A burr is a prickly seed or plant part that sticks to anything it touches, like your clothes, your pet's fur, or your shoelaces when you walk through tall grass), "Yo, what if we made something like this?" And **boom** — now we've got Velcro everywhere, from sneakers to space gear!

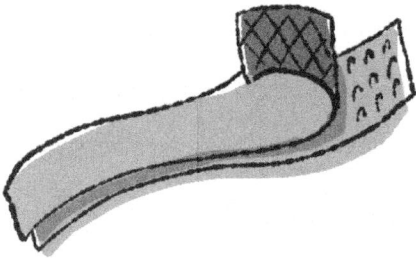

Bullet trains: Engineers were trying to make *bullet trains* faster and quieter, so they looked at the *kingfisher bird.* Why? Because this bird dives into water at high speed with barely a

splash. They copied its beak shape for the front of the train, making it way quieter and more efficient. Talk about next-level inspiration!

Wind turbines: Even *wind turbines* are taking cues from nature. The fins of *humpback whales* have little bumps (called tubercles) that help them glide better through water. Engineers thought, *"What if we use that on wind turbine blades?"* and it worked! Now turbines catch wind more efficiently, thanks to some whale wisdom.

Nature's been slaying the problem-solving game for millions of years, so why not let it help us out? With biomimicry, we can create inventions that are smarter, faster, and more eco-friendly by using nature's genius designs. It's like learning from the *GOAT* of engineering — *Mother Nature* herself!

FUN FACT: AIRPLANES? Yep, they were inspired by birds! The Wright brothers watched birds to figure out how to control flight. So, every time you hop on a plane, remember it's got bird vibes helping it soar!

With biomimicry, the next big invention could literally be chilling in your backyard. Nature's got all the best ideas — you just gotta catch them!

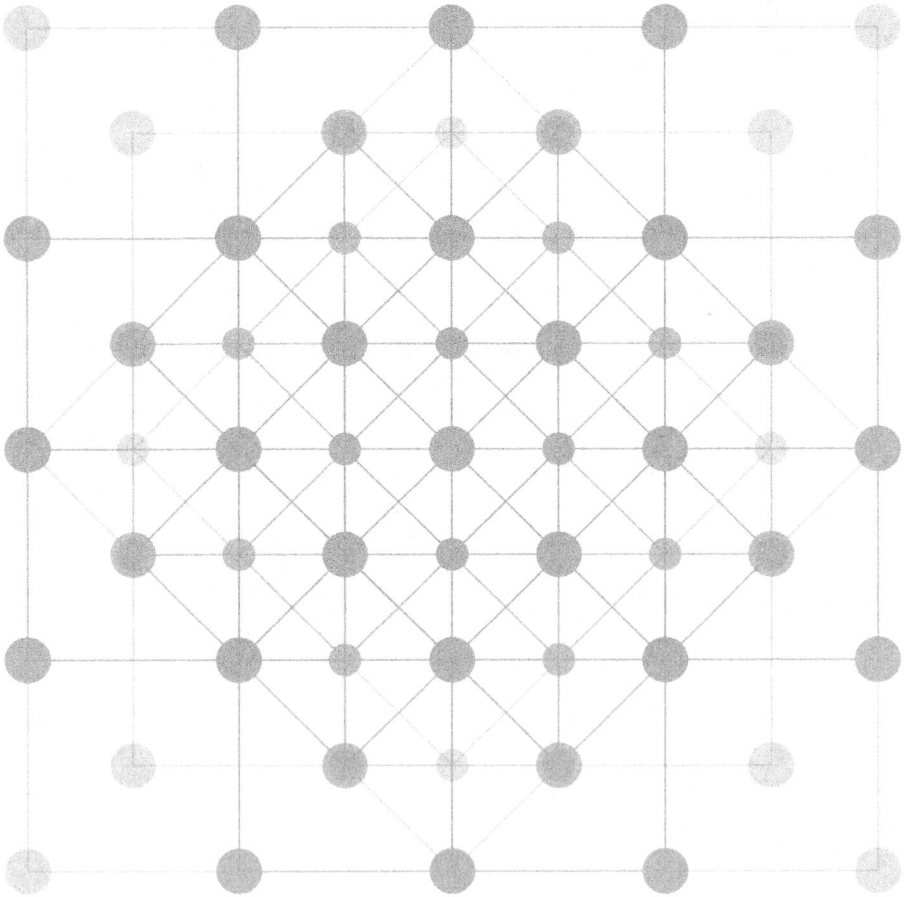

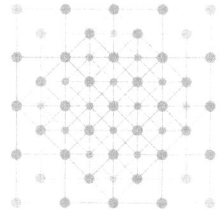

SPACE EXPLORATION

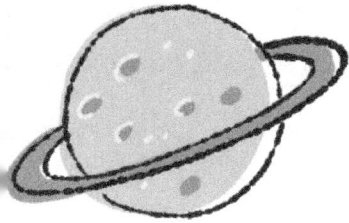

HOW DO STARS AND PLANETS FORM?

Alright, so stars and planets forming is basically the OG glow-up in the universe. It all starts in these massive clouds of gas and dust, called nebulae. Picture this: gravity starts pulling all that stuff together, and as it clumps up, things heat up—like, really heat up. Once the gas gets super hot and dense, **BOOM** — a star is born! It's like the universe's ultimate fusion reactor, with the star burning for billions of years.

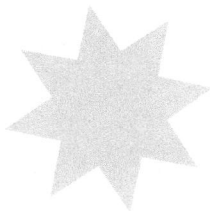

Planets? They're the next part of the story. Around these new stars, leftover bits of gas, rock, and ice start clumping together, spinning around in a protoplanetary disk. Over time, these clumps get bigger and bigger, smashing into each other until, bam, you've got planets forming. Some stay rocky like *Earth*, and others gather up gas to become giants like *Jupiter*. It's like cosmic Legos, but way cooler.

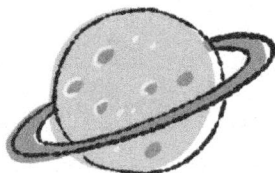

And here's the kicker: this whole process takes millions of years. So, next time you look up at the stars, just remember they went through a massive cosmic glow-up to get there—and we're lucky to be part of the squad in this huge universe!

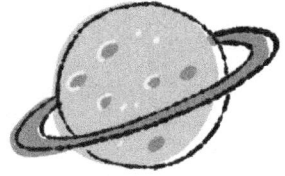

FUN FACT: Did you know that stars actually have "life cycles"? They're born, live for billions of years, and then die in epic ways! Some stars end their lives with a bang—literally—as supernovas, which are massive explosions that can outshine entire galaxies for a short time. And if the star was super massive, it might even collapse into a black hole. Talk about going out with a bang!

HOW DO ASTRONAUTS SLEEP IN SPACE?

Sleeping in space is definitely not like crashing in your bed at home! There's no gravity, so astronauts can't just lie down like we do on Earth. Instead, they sleep in sleeping bags that are strapped to the walls or ceilings of their spacecraft, so they don't float around like balloons. These sleeping bags keep them snug and in place while they snooze.

Even though there's no comfy mattress, astronauts still get 8 hours of sleep just like us. And since there's no up or down in space, it doesn't really matter where they *"lie down."* They can sleep standing up, sideways, or floating — it's all the same in *zero gravity*!

Plus, the *International Space Station (ISS)* orbits Earth about every 90 minutes, so astronauts see 16 sunrises and sunsets a day! To avoid getting confused by the constant changes, they use special eye masks or cover their sleeping area to block out light and stick to a regular sleep schedule.

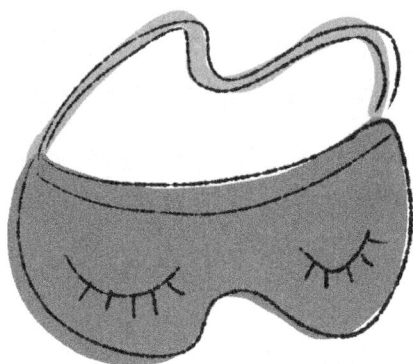

FUN FACT: Some astronauts say they actually sleep better in space because zero gravity takes all the pressure off their bodies — no sore backs or necks! Now that's some next-level relaxation!

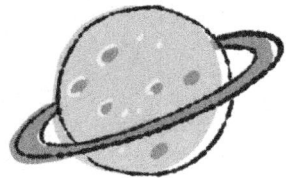

WHY DOESN'T THE SUN BURN OUT?

The Sun isn't your average fire — it's basically a giant nuclear reactor floating in space. Instead of burning wood or fuel like a bonfire, the Sun's powered by nuclear fusion. This is where it takes a bunch of hydrogen atoms, smashes them together, and turns them into helium. When that happens, a crazy amount of energy is released, which is what makes the Sun shine so bright and keep us all warm.

Now, you might be wondering, "*How long can the Sun keep this up?*" Well, the Sun's got plenty of hydrogen — enough to keep the party going for another 5 billion years. It's been shining for about *4.6 billion years* already, so it's not running out of fuel anytime soon.

When the Sun does start to run low on hydrogen, it's not just gonna flicker out. Nope! It'll swell up into a red giant, which could swallow up some of the inner planets (*RIP, Mercury and Venus*). After that, it'll shrink down into a white dwarf, which is like the Sun's final form—a tiny, super-dense leftover. But don't worry, that's not happening for a long, long time.

FUN FACT: Even though the Sun is constantly burning through hydrogen, it only loses a tiny amount of its mass over billions of years. So, no need to panic—we've got plenty of sunshine left to enjoy!

CAN WE LIVE ON MARS ONE DAY?

Living on Mars would be next-level wild! First off, we'd have to stay in domes or live underground because there's no chill atmosphere like Earth's. Mars doesn't have enough air for us to breathe, and the radiation from the Sun is no joke. So, no going outside without a space suit unless you're cool with being crispy!

We'd have to grow food in some high-tech greenhouses, using Martian soil mixed with all kinds of nutrients. And water? We'd probably have to melt ice from Mars or get really good at recycling it. Talk about living off the grid!

Mars' gravity is way weaker than Earth's, so you'd feel super light. You could literally jump higher and carry heavy stuff like a boss. But, real talk — low gravity might mess with your muscles, so you'd be hitting the gym a lot just to stay in shape.

It's also freezing on Mars, like -80°F on the regular — so, no more complaining about cold weather on Earth! You'd need heated gear and suits to even step outside, and don't forget about those epic dust storms. They can last for weeks and cover entire regions of the planet.

Oh, and here's a weird flex: a day on Mars is just a bit longer than an Earth day *(about 24.6 hours)*, but a year is almost double what we're used to — *687 Earth days!* So, birthdays on Mars? Way fewer of them!

Living on Mars would definitely be an adventure, but it'd take a lot of tech and hustle to make it work. Still, you'd be part of history living on another planet—how lit is that?

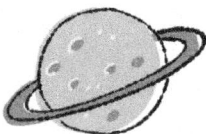

HOW DO ASTRONAUTS GO TO THE BATHROOM IN SPACE?

Alright, so going to the bathroom in space is not your regular pit stop. Without gravity, stuff doesn't just "flush" down like it does on Earth. Everything floats, so astronauts need some seriously next-level tech to keep things under control!

They use special space toilets that come with a built-in vacuum system — basically, a space-age suction system to pull everything down. For liquid waste, astronauts use a funnel attached to a hose, and the vacuum sucks it away. For solid waste, they sit on a toilet with straps (yes, seatbelts for your butt!) to hold them down, and the vacuum handles the rest.

Now here's the wild part: the pee? They recycle it into *drinking water!* Yeah, you heard that right — they purify it so they can reuse it. It might sound kinda sus, but in space, every drop counts, and this system makes sure astronauts stay hydrated without wasting water. It's basically space-level zero waste living!

As for solid waste, it gets packed up in special containers and either sent back to Earth or tossed into space to burn up in the atmosphere like a mini meteor shower. So while space might look all glamorous, even astronauts gotta deal with the basics — but they're doing it in style!

WHY DO ASTRONAUTS NEED SPACESUITS?

Spacesuits are like the ultimate survival gear for astronauts. If you tried stepping into space without one, you'd be toast — literally! Space is no joke: no air, extreme temperatures, and intense radiation. A spacesuit is basically a mini spaceship that you wear, packed with everything you need to stay alive out there.

First off, spacesuits give astronauts *oxygen* to breathe. Space has zero air, so without that oxygen supply, an astronaut wouldn't last more than a few seconds. The suit has built-in oxygen tanks that feed air through the helmet, keeping them breathing easy.

Next, there's the whole temperature thing. Space can swing from freezing cold *(like -250°F)* in the shadows to scorching hot *(up to 250°F)* in the sunlight. Spacesuits regulate body temperature with special layers that either trap heat or release it. Imagine stepping into both a freezer and an oven — yeah, the suit has to handle all of that!

Another key feature? *Pressure*. On Earth, we have air pressure that keeps our bodies in check. In space, there's none of that, and without a suit, an astronaut's body would swell up because fluids in their body would expand. The spacesuit creates just the right amount of pressure to keep their bodies from ballooning out.

Let's not forget about the *radiation*. Earth's atmosphere protects us from dangerous cosmic rays, but in space, astronauts are exposed to radiation from the Sun and other stars. Spacesuits have special layers that help block this harmful radiation, keeping astronauts safe from what's basically space's version of a sunburn — on steroids!

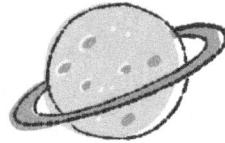

Spacesuits also come with a helmet visor that's like wearing the best *pair of sunglasses* ever. The visor protects astronauts' eyes from the blinding light of the Sun, which in space is way more intense than we experience on Earth. Plus, spacesuits have

communication systems built in, so astronauts can chat with their crew or mission control back on Earth while they're out doing their spacewalks. Imagine working on a spaceship 250 miles above Earth and still being able to say, *"Hey, can you hear me now?"*

Fun Fact: the backpack on the spacesuit? That's called the Portable Life Support System, and it's not just for show—it provides oxygen, removes carbon dioxide, controls temperature, and holds the communication gear. It's like wearing a life support machine, air conditioner, and Wi-Fi router all in one!

NATURE & ANIMALS

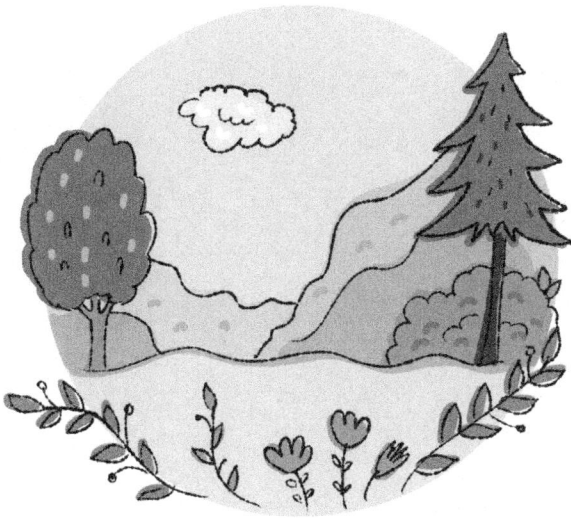

HOW DO JELLYFISH GLOW IN THE DARK?

Jellyfish have one of the coolest superpowers in the ocean — they can glow in the dark! This glowing is called bioluminescence, and it's like nature's built-in nightlight. But how does it work?

Inside some jellyfish, there are special proteins called luciferins. When these proteins mix with oxygen, they give off light. It's kind of like a chemical reaction party happening inside the jellyfish! This glow can be blue, green, or even red, depending on the jellyfish species and where they live in the ocean.

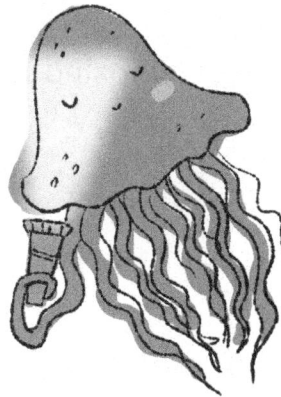

But why do jellyfish glow? They use their glow-up for a few reasons:

Defense: Some jellyfish light up to scare off predators. A sudden burst of light can confuse or startle whatever's trying to eat them.

Camouflage: In the deep ocean, where it's pitch black, glowing can help jellyfish blend in or even hide from enemies by matching the light coming from above.

Hunting: Some jellyfish use their glow to attract prey. Smaller creatures might swim toward the light, thinking it's food, but instead, they get trapped by the jellyfish's stinging tentacles.

FUN FACT: Scientists have actually used jellyfish bioluminescence to create a glowing protein called GFP (Green Fluorescent Protein), which is now used in labs all over the world for medical research. Jellyfish glow is helping humans make some big discoveries!

When you next see a glowing jellyfish, just know they're flexing their natural glow-up for some pretty epic reasons!

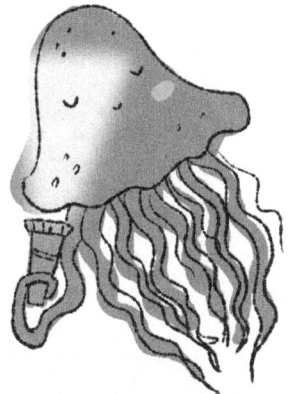

WHAT'S THE STRONGEST ANIMAL ON EARTH?

Believe it or not, the strongest animal on Earth isn't an elephant or a gorilla — it's the tiny dung beetle! Yep, this little bug might be small, but it has some serious strength. The *dung beetle* can pull, push, and carry loads that are up to 1,000 times its own body weight. Imagine you being able to carry a whole stack of cars — that's what it's like for a dung beetle!

These bugs use their incredible strength to roll and bury dung (*aka poop*), which they use for food and a place to lay their eggs. Their strength comes in handy when they have to move dung balls across tough terrain or fight off other beetles trying to steal their prize.

Even though dung beetles aren't big like elephants, pound for pound, they're the strongest animal on the planet!

FUN FACT: In the human world, if you had the strength of a dung beetle, you'd be able to lift 10 elephants at once! How's that for a superpower?

WHY DO BIRDS FLY SOUTH FOR THE WINTER?

Birds fly south for the winter because they're all about chasing that warm weather and keeping their bellies full. When winter hits in places up north, things get freezing, and their usual food sources, like insects and berries, disappear. Instead of sticking around and toughing it out, birds decide to peace out and head south to where the sun's still shining, and there's plenty to eat.

This huge move is called migration, and some birds really go all out. We're talking about flights that cover thousands of miles. For example, the Arctic tern is basically the *MVP of migration*, traveling more than *11,000 miles* to get from *the Arctic* all the way to *Antarctica*. That's like crossing the globe — and then some — just to hang out in warmer weather!

But it's not just about the vibes and good weather. Migration helps birds find the best spots to rest, feed, and stay away from predators during the winter. It's like their version of a tropical vacation. When spring rolls around and the weather warms up back home, they make the trek north again, ready for the summer scene.

FUN FACT: Some birds, like the bar-tailed godwit, can fly non-stop for 7,000 miles without taking a break. No mid-flight snacks, no pit stops—just pure dedication. That's a next-level endurance challenge!

The next time you see birds flying south in formation, just know they're off on an epic journey to avoid the cold and soak up the sun. They've got that ultimate snowbird lifestyle down!

WHAT'S THE FASTEST CREATURE ON LAND?

The fastest creature on land is *the cheetah*, and this big cat is the real *MVP of speed*. Cheetahs can hit speeds of up to *70 miles per hour* (that's faster than most cars on the highway!) in just a few seconds. They're like the sports cars of the animal kingdom, with incredible acceleration and agility.

But here's the thing — cheetahs can't keep that speed up for long. They're sprinters, not marathon runners. After a short burst of speed, usually about *20 to 30 seconds*, they have to slow down to catch their breath. During that time, they cover up to *500 meters* while chasing down prey like gazelles or other fast animals.

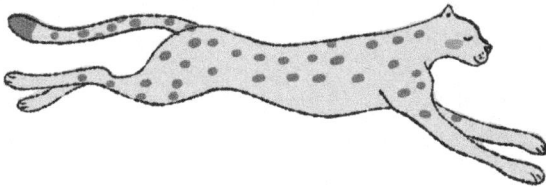

The secret to their speed? Cheetahs have super flexible spines that act like a spring, long legs, and non-retractable claws that help them grip the ground like running spikes. Their entire body is built for speed, from their lightweight frame to their long tail, which helps them steer like a race car driver at high speeds.

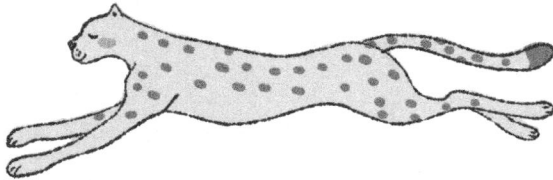

FUN FACT: Even though cheetahs are crazy fast, they need to be super precise with their hunts because if they don't catch their prey quickly, they'll run out of energy fast. So, they're not just speed demons—they're also master strategists!

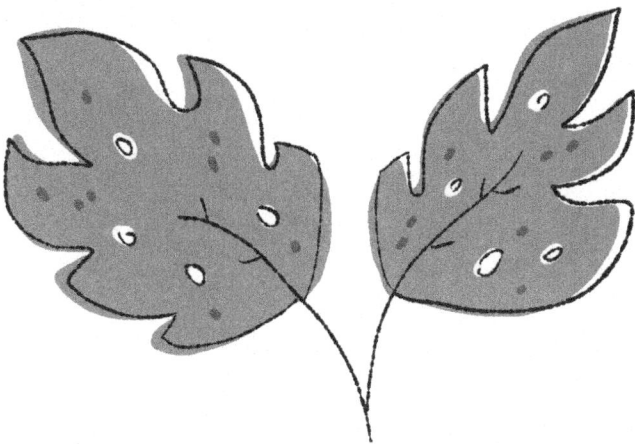

WHAT'S ON THE INSIDE OF A TURTLE'S SHELL?

A turtle's shell isn't just a hard backpack they can hop in and out of — it's literally part of their body! The top part is called the carapace, and the bottom is the plastron, and both are actually fused to the turtle's spine and ribs. *So, it's like they're wearing their skeleton on the outside!*

Inside the shell, they've got all their important organs — like their heart, lungs, and stomach — tucked away nice and safe. The shell acts like their personal suit of armor, keeping them protected. But here's the thing: it's not all cozy and roomy like our homes with a warm bed and TV to chill in. Turtles don't get that level of comfort! Instead, they have to work with what they've got — an armored crib that's cool for protection but not exactly luxury living.

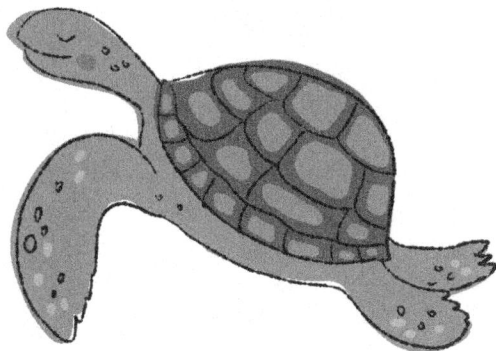

115

Also, since their ribs are part of the shell, they don't breathe the way we do. They have special muscles inside that help them inhale and exhale, which is pretty unique. And yep, turtles can actually feel their shells because they've got nerves in there, so they know when something's touching them, even though the outside is super hard.

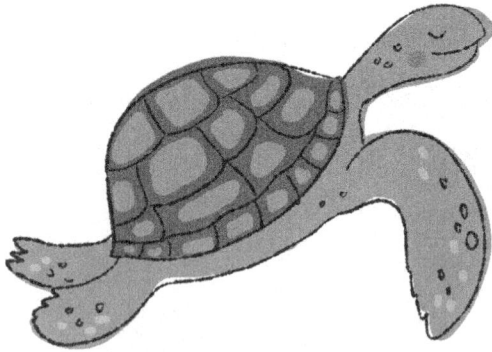

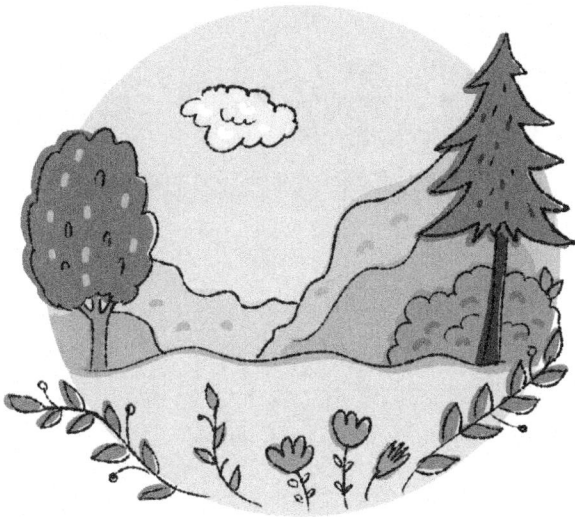

CAN PLANTS TALK TO EACH OTHER?

Believe it or not, plants have their own sneaky way of "*talking*"! While they don't chat like we do, they've got a whole system of sending chemical signals and using their roots to communicate — it's like they're part of an *underground Wi-Fi network!*

Here's the lowdown: when a plant is under attack, like if some bug is munching on its leaves, it can send out chemical distress signals into the air. Other plants nearby pick up these signals and go into defense mode, cranking out chemicals that make them taste nasty to the bugs. It's like a plant version of "*Yo, heads up! Trouble's coming!*"

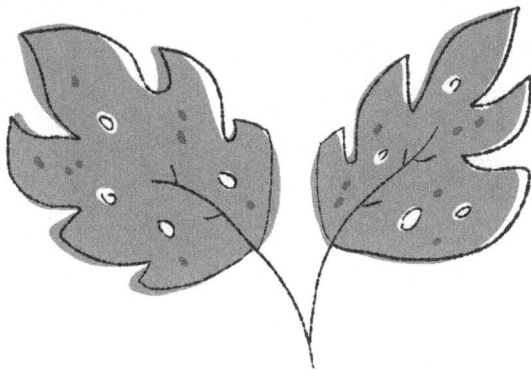

But the coolest part? Plants also "talk" through their roots. They use a network of fungi underground called *the Wood Wide Web* (yep, that's the real name!). These fungi connect plant roots like a super secret chatroom, letting them share resources like water and nutrients. So, if one plant is struggling, it can hit up its neighbors for help, and they'll send some extra nutrients or water.

FUN FACT: Willow trees are like the drama queens of the plant world! When bugs start snacking on their leaves, they send out distress signals, and other willows nearby get the message and start prepping their defenses. It's like they're all out here looking out for the squad.

So, while plants aren't chatting in words, they've definitely got their own high-key ways of staying connected and looking out for each other in their own plant network!

WHY DO BEES USE HEXAGONS TO BUILD THEIR HIVES?

Bees are total *math wizards!* They build their hives out of *hexagons* because it's the most efficient shape around. Using hexagons lets them store the most honey while using the least amount of wax. Basically, bees figured out the ultimate life hack for saving energy and space!

Here's the scoop: hexagons fit together perfectly without leaving any gaps, which makes the hive super strong and allows the bees to pack in as much honey as possible. Plus, hexagons use less wax than other shapes, so the bees don't have to work as hard making wax and can spend more time making honey. It's like they've got nature's version of a pro storage system!

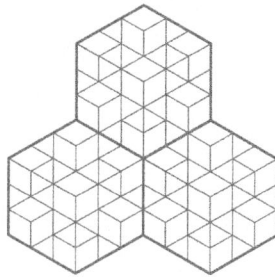

FUN FACT: Humans have borrowed this trick from bees using biomimicry! Engineers and designers use the hexagon shape in all kinds of things — from building materials to packing designs — because it's super strong and space-efficient. Bees have been rocking this design for millions of years, and now humans are copying their genius moves!

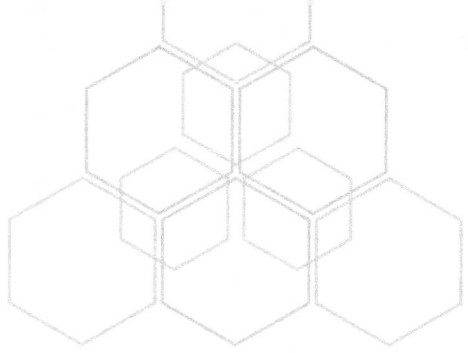

Not only are bees making honey, but they're also low-key inspiring human engineers with their epic geometry skills!

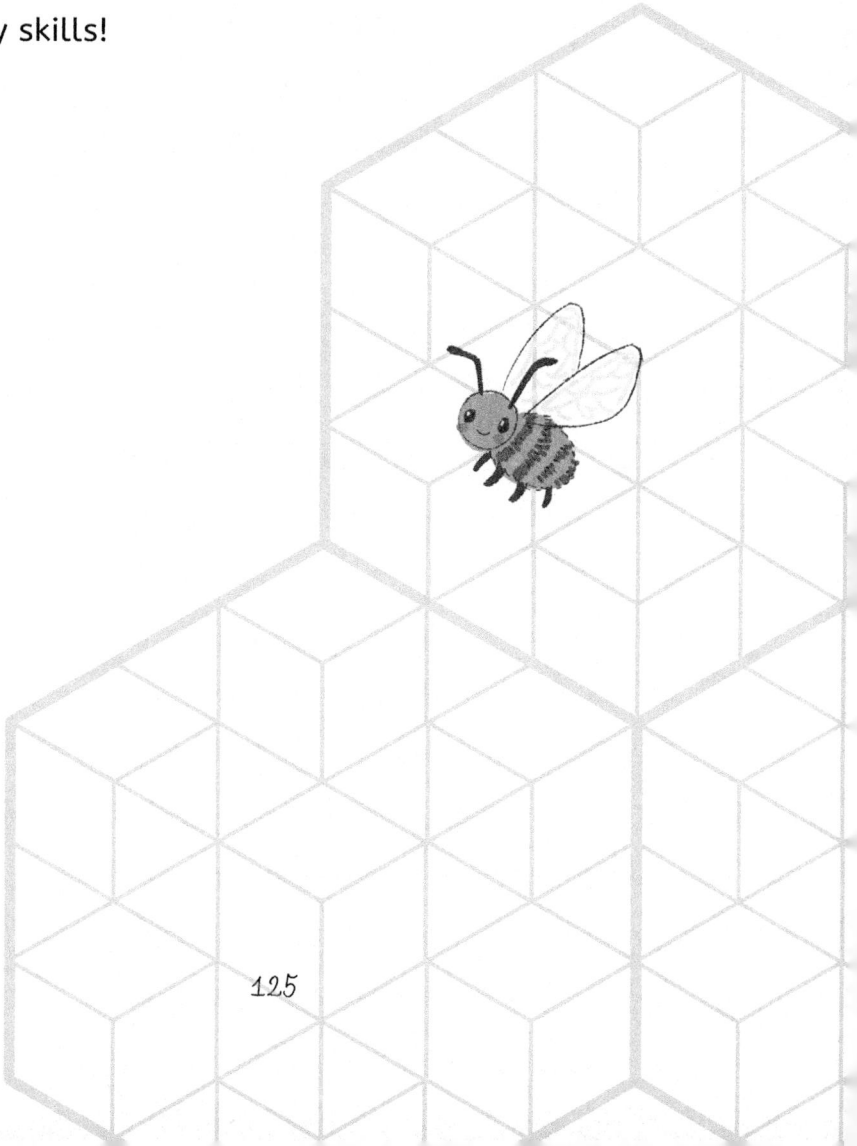

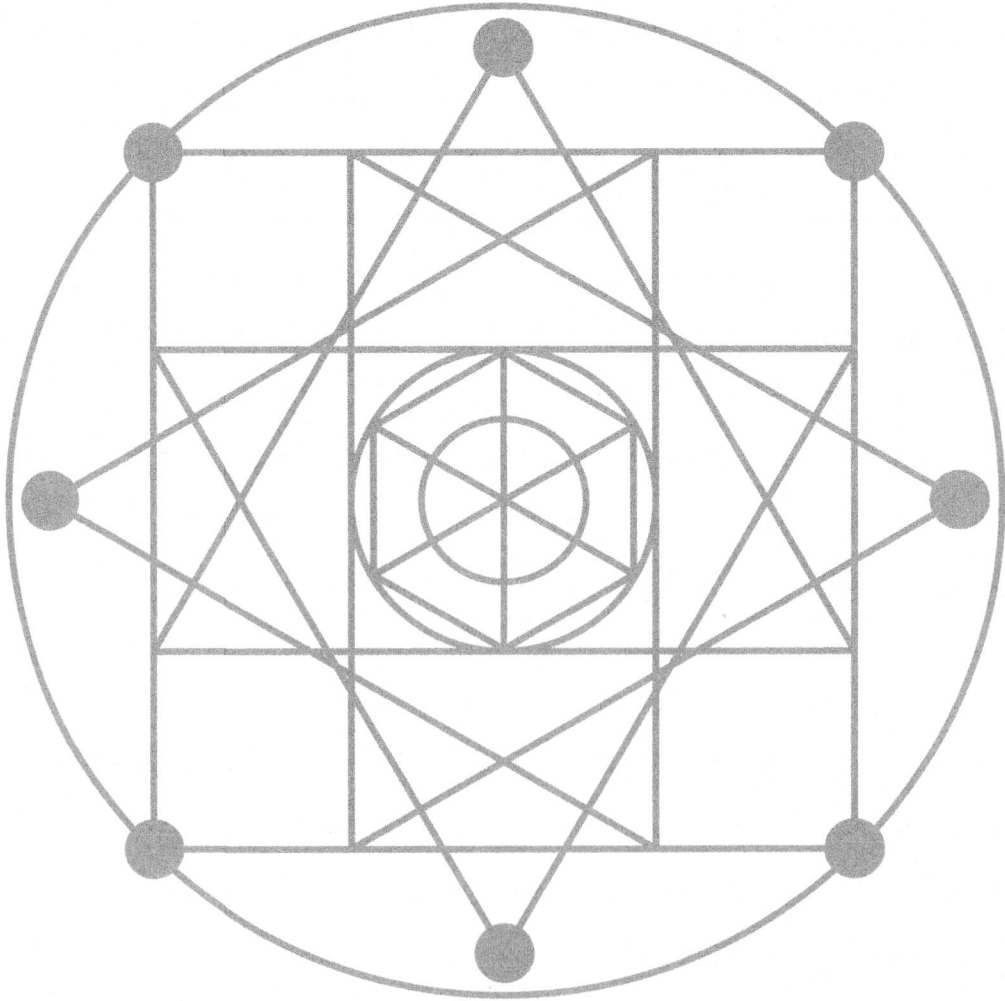

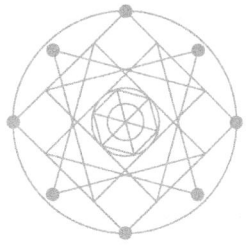

HUMAN BODY & HEALTH

WHY IS MY SNOT YELLOW WHEN I'M SICK?

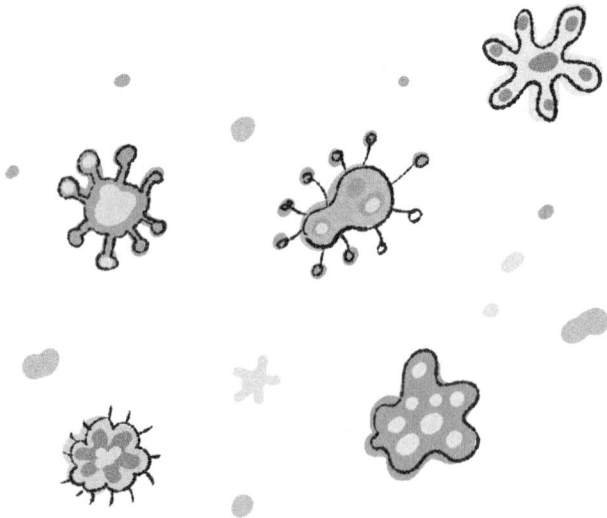

When you're sick and your snot turns all yellow, it's your body going full-on defense mode against the germs that are messing with you. Here's how it works: when your body detects a virus or bacteria (like *a cold or infection*), it sends in the white blood cell squad to fight the invaders. These white blood cells are like your body's superheroes, rushing to the scene to destroy the germs causing trouble.

As your immune system fights back, some of those white blood cells and other infection-fighting cells get tired and break down. The mix of dead cells, bacteria, and proteins is what gives your snot that lovely yellow tint. So yeah, your snot turning yellow is actually a sign that your body's immune system is in full beast mode fighting to get you better!

If your snot turns green, that's usually a sign that the battle is getting even more intense! Your immune system is working overtime to knock out the infection, and the green color comes from the extra iron in certain white blood cells. It might look nasty, but it's actually a sign that your body's putting in the work.

The thicker your snot gets, the more dried-out your mucus is becoming. This happens when you're a little dehydrated, so keep drinking water to help thin things out and flush out the gunk!

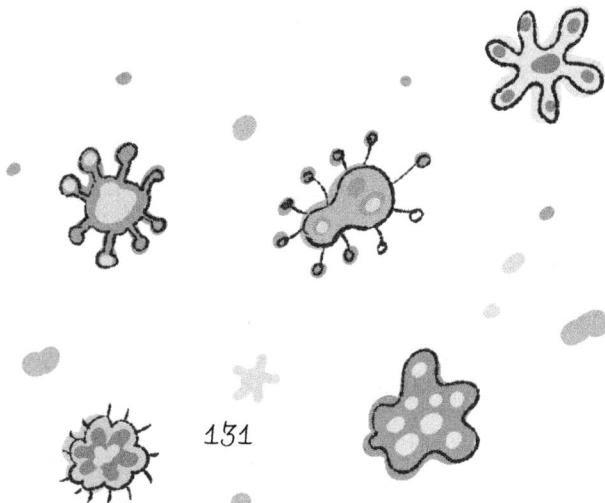

131

HOW DO MUSCLES GROW WHEN WE EXERCISE?

When you hit the gym, play sports, or even do some push-ups at home, your muscles are actually getting a workout in more ways than one. Here's the breakdown: when you exercise, especially doing things like lifting weights or bodyweight exercises, you're putting stress on your muscles. This causes tiny tears in the muscle fibers — don't worry, it sounds bad, but it's actually a good thing!

After your workout, your body goes into repair mode. It sends nutrients, like protein, to the muscle fibers to fix those tiny tears. But instead of just fixing them back to normal, your body makes the muscles stronger and bigger to handle the stress better next time. This process is called muscle hypertrophy — basically, it's like upgrading your muscles with every workout!

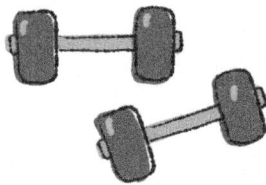

The key to muscle growth is giving your body time to rest and recover. When you sleep and eat foods rich in protein, like chicken, eggs, and beans, your body uses those building blocks to help grow your muscles. That's why it's super important to balance hard workouts with proper rest and good nutrition.

FUN FACT: Your muscles don't grow while you're working out—they actually grow when you're resting and recovering afterward. So if you're all about building muscle, make sure to get plenty of sleep and protein to help your body repair and grow!

Every time you exercise and challenge your muscles, you're basically sending them a message: "Let's get stronger!" And with enough time, rest, and the right fuel, your muscles will do just that.

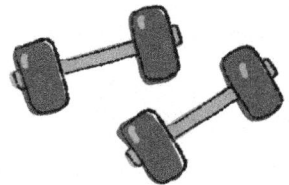

WHY DO WE GET GOOSEBUMPS?

Goosebumps are your body's way of saying, "*Whoa, something's going down!*" Whether you're feeling cold, freaked out, or super hyped, it's all thanks to these tiny muscles at the base of each hair on your skin called the arrector pili muscles. When those muscles tighten up, your hair stands on end, and your skin gets that *bumpy, chicken-skin* look — aka, *goosebumps!*

Here's why it happens: Back in the day, when humans were way hairier, goosebumps were actually useful. If it got cold, the hair standing up would trap air and keep you warmer. If you were scared, the hair would puff up to make you look bigger and tougher, like, "*Don't mess with me!*" It was nature's way of throwing up a defense mode.

Nowadays, we don't have as much body hair, so goosebumps are kind of just leftovers from our ancient survival toolkit. But your body still kicks into goosebump mode when you're cold or feeling some type of way — whether it's fear, excitement, or just a killer song that gives you all the feels.

So yeah, while goosebumps might not keep you warm or scare off enemies anymore, they're still your body's throwback reaction to something big happening — whether it's cold air or a major mood!

FUN FACT: You can get goosebumps when you're hyped or emotional, too! That's why you might catch them when watching an epic movie scene, hearing a crazy good song, or even having a deep convo. Your body's like, "This is intense, let's crank up the goosebumps!"

WHAT MAKES OUR HEART BEAT FASTER WHEN WE'RE SCARED?

When you get scared, your body goes into *fight-or-flight mode*, and things get real intense, real fast. Your brain senses danger and sends out a distress signal to a little part called the *amygdala* (the *"fear center"* of your brain). The amygdala then tells your body to release adrenaline, which is like nature's ultimate energy drink.

Adrenaline gets your heart pumping faster, which helps send extra oxygen and blood to your muscles. It's like your body is gearing up to either fight whatever is scaring you or make a fast escape. Your heart's racing to make sure you're ready for action, whether you're running from a spooky noise or getting through a haunted house!

Adrenaline also causes other things to happen, like making you breathe faster and giving you that butterflies-in-the-stomach feeling. It's all part of your body's ancient survival instincts to help you react quickly and stay alert.

FUN FACT: Your fight-or-flight response is super quick, sometimes kicking in before you even realize what's happening. It's the reason your heart starts pounding the moment something freaks you out—even if it's just a jump scare in a movie!

So, when your heart's racing during a scary moment, it's your body going, "*We need to be ready for anything,*" whether that means fighting, fleeing, or just getting through the fright!

WHY DO WE DREAM WHEN WE SLEEP?

Dreams are like your brain's nightly highlight reel, playing while you're snoozing. When you sleep, especially during a stage called REM sleep (Rapid Eye Movement), your brain is still super active, even though your body is resting. It's during this REM stage that most of your dreams happen.

So, why do we dream? Well, scientists aren't 100% sure, but there are a few popular theories. One idea is that dreams help us process emotions and memories from the day. It's like your brain sorting through everything that happened, filing away the important stuff, and sometimes throwing in some random, trippy details just for fun!

Another theory is that dreams let your brain practice for real-life situations. Ever have a dream where you're running from something or solving a problem? Your brain might be prepping you for potential challenges, kind of like a mental rehearsal for real-world scenarios.

So, while we're still figuring out the full "why" behind dreams, they're like your brain's way of hitting "play" on some pretty wild mental movies while you rest up!

FUN FACT: You can have multiple dreams in one night, even if you don't remember most of them! The average person spends about 2 hours dreaming every night, whether it's an epic adventure or just some weird, random scenes.

HOW DO VACCINES HELP US STAY HEALTHY?

Vaccines are like training programs for your immune system, helping your body learn how to fight off certain germs without you actually getting sick. Here's how it works: when you get a vaccine, it introduces a tiny, harmless part of a virus or bacteria into your body. This is usually a weakened or dead version of the germ, or sometimes just a small piece of it, like a protein.

Your immune system sees this and goes, "Whoa, what's this?" and starts creating antibodies, which are like the body's defense soldiers. These antibodies learn how to recognize and fight off the invader. But since the vaccine doesn't make you sick, it's like a practice run for your immune system to get stronger.

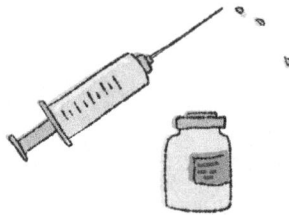

Then, if the real virus or bacteria ever shows up, your body's already prepped and knows exactly how to defeat it. The antibodies remember the bad guy and jump into action, taking it down before it can cause a full-blown infection.

Vaccines don't just protect you — they also help protect the people around you! This is called herd immunity, where if enough people are vaccinated, it makes it harder for germs to spread, protecting those who can't get vaccinated, like newborns or people with certain health conditions.

Vaccines are like your body's secret weapon, giving your immune system the tools it needs to stay ahead of the game and keep you healthy without having to fight off the real deal!

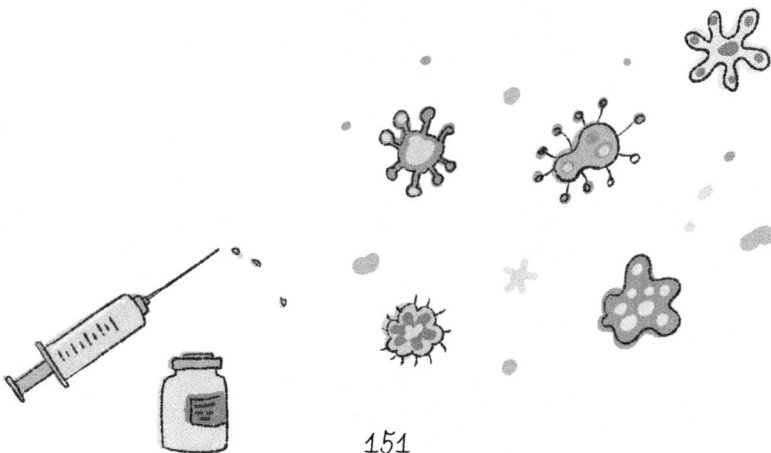

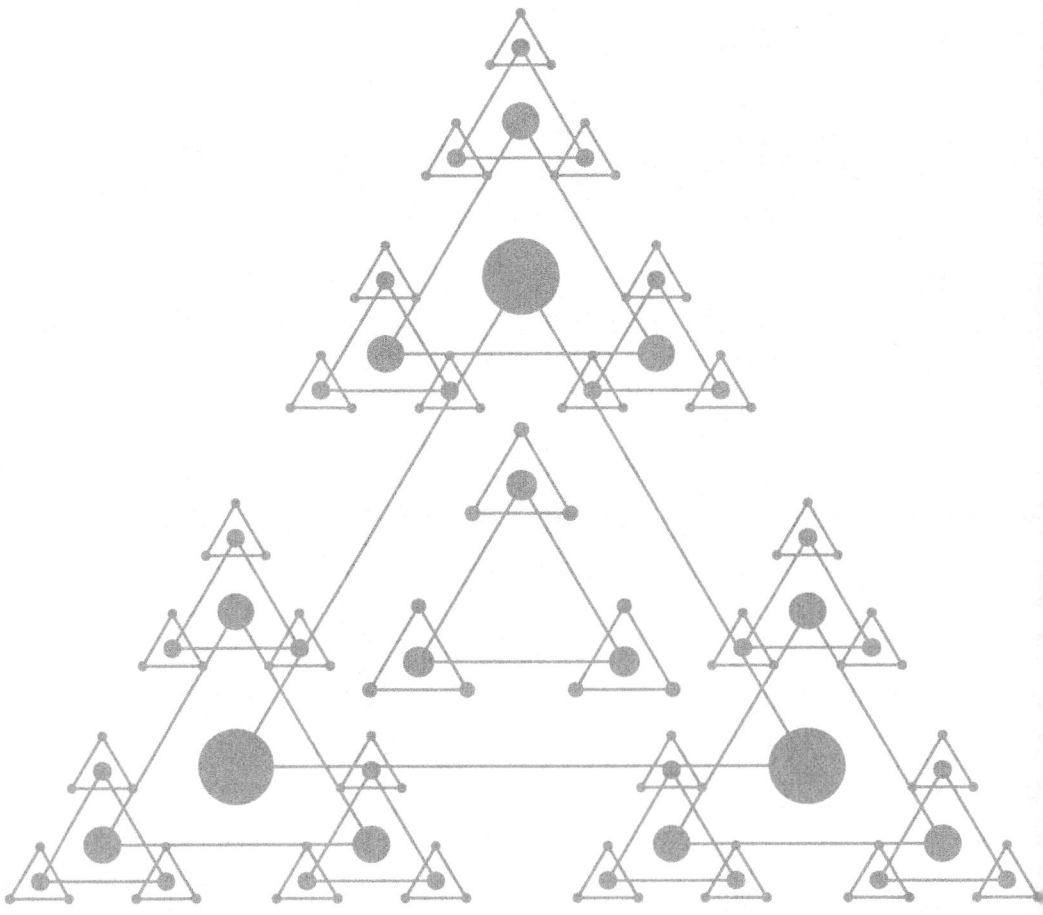

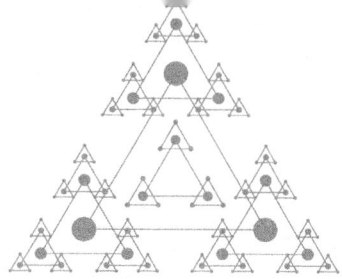

WEIRD-BUT-TRUE FACTS

HOW MANY COLORS CAN THE HUMAN EYE SEE?

The human eye can see around *10 million colors!* That's right — our eyes are pretty impressive. They have special cells called cones, and there are three types of cones, each tuned to a specific color: red, green, and blue. These cones work together like a color-mixing team, blending different amounts of red, green, and blue to create all the shades we see. It's like having a built-in color lab in your eyes.

Light hits objects, and depending on what color that object is, it reflects certain wavelengths of light back to your eyes. The cones detect those wavelengths, send signals to your brain, and then — **bam!** — you see color. That's why a red apple looks red, and the blue sky looks blue.

Some people, called tetrachromats, have an extra cone in their eyes. This means they can see up to 100 million colors, way more than the average person! Imagine seeing colors in a whole new dimension — what looks like a regular shade of green to you could be a mix of unique hues to them.

Also, there are conditions like color blindness where people have fewer functioning cones, so they can't see as many colors, and certain shades like red and green might look similar. Even though they see the world differently, they still experience it in awesome ways!

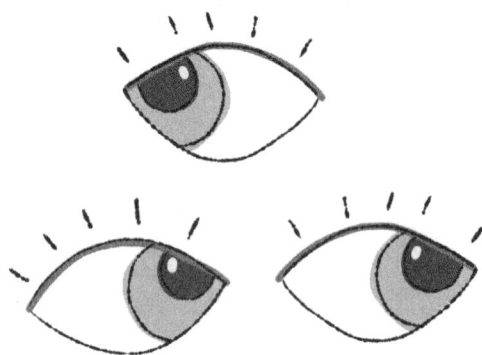

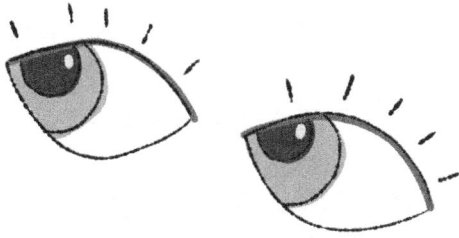

With all that color vision power, it's wild to think about how much our eyes can pick up — from the tiniest difference between two shades of blue to the full spectrum of a rainbow.

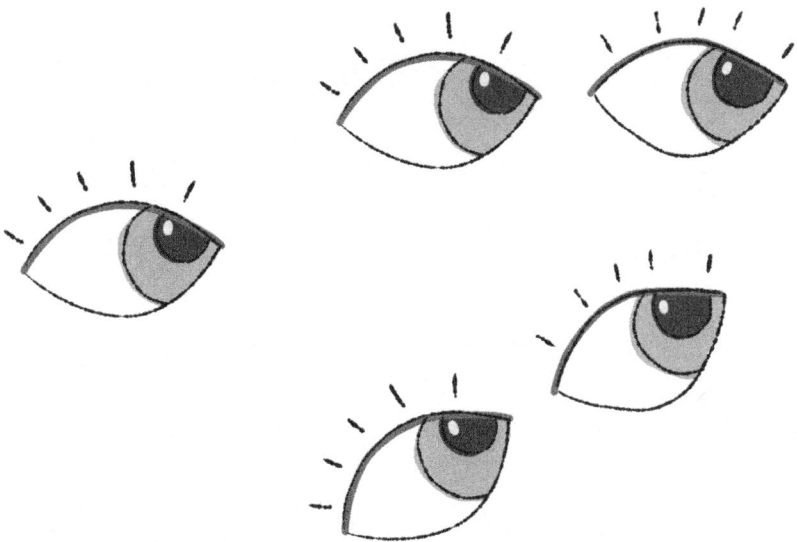

WHY DO FIREFLIES LIGHT UP?

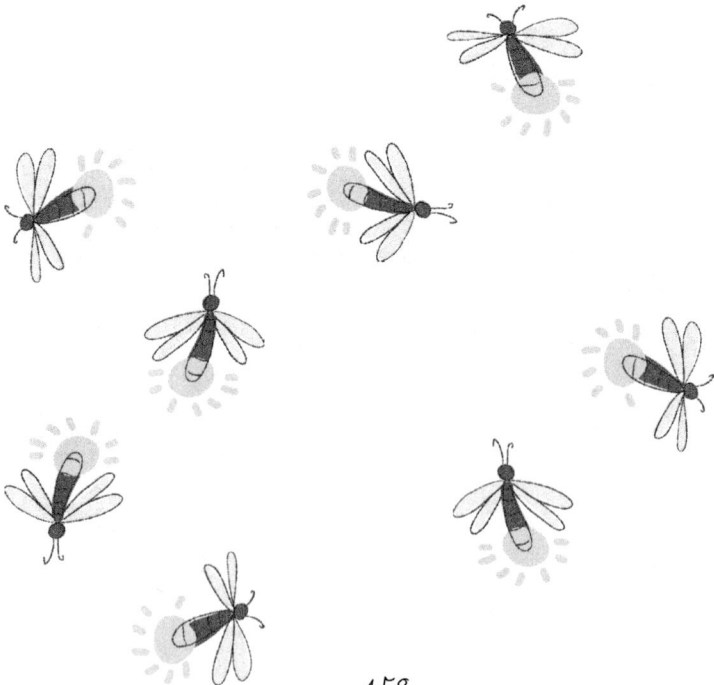

158

Fireflies light up thanks to a cool chemical reaction happening inside their bodies, called bioluminescence. It's like nature's version of glow-in-the-dark magic! Inside their lower abdomen, fireflies mix a special chemical called luciferin with oxygen, an enzyme called luciferase, and a little bit of energy. When all of these ingredients combine, they produce that iconic glow.

But why do fireflies light up? They use their glow for a few different reasons:

Attracting mates: Male fireflies flash patterns of light to show off and get the attention of female fireflies. Each species of firefly has its own unique light pattern, so it's like their version of sending out a custom text or snap!

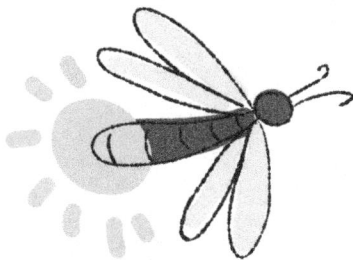

Defense: Some fireflies use their glow to warn predators that they don't taste very good or are toxic. It's like having a built-in warning sign that says, "Stay away!"

Communication: Fireflies can also use their light to communicate with each other in different ways. Whether it's finding a mate or signaling danger, their glow helps them connect in the dark.

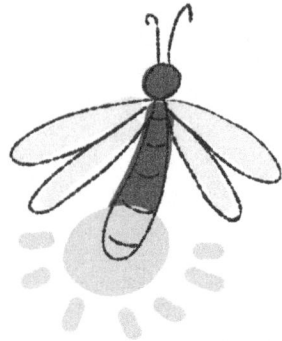

FUN FACT: Fireflies are so efficient at making light that almost all the energy from their chemical reaction is turned into light. In comparison, a regular light bulb wastes a lot of energy as heat. Fireflies are basically glowing energy savers!

Their glowing bodies make them one of the most magical creatures in nature's light show, and they light up summer nights with style.

WHY DO SOME ANIMALS NEVER NEED TO DRINK WATER?

Some animals have evolved to live in super dry places where water is hard to come by, so they've figured out a way to survive without ever needing to drink! These animals get all the water they need from the food they eat or even from the air. Their bodies are like ultimate water-saving machines, able to make the most of every drop.

Take the *kangaroo rat*, for example. This little desert dweller lives in some of the driest places on Earth but never drinks water. Instead, it gets all its moisture from the seeds it munches on. Even better, its body is super efficient at conserving water. Kangaroo rats have kidneys that can extract every bit of water from their food, and they produce almost no waste moisture (their pee is super concentrated, like tiny drops of syrup!).

163

Another example is the *thorny devil lizard* from Australia. This lizard has the crazy ability to absorb water through its skin! Its body is covered in grooves that funnel dew and moisture from the air straight to its mouth. It's like having a built-in water collection system.

FUN FACT: Some animals, like the Namib desert beetle, can collect water from fog! It stands still and lets moisture from the fog condense on its back, which then trickles down to its mouth—literally drinking the air!

These animals have adapted to live in extreme conditions, making them the ultimate water-conservation experts. Whether through food, air, or their unique bodies, they've found creative ways to stay hydrated without ever needing to take a sip!

165

WHY DO ONIONS MAKE US CRY?

Onions have a sneaky defense mechanism that kicks in when you cut into them, and that's what makes you tear up. Inside an onion are special compounds that stay separated until you start slicing. When you cut into the onion, these compounds mix together and create a gas called syn-Propanethial-S-oxide (yep, that's a mouthful!). This gas floats up into the air and heads straight for your eyes.

When the gas hits your eyes, it reacts with the water in your tears and forms a mild acid. Your eyes don't like this acid at all, so they start to tear up to flush out the irritant. It's like your body's way of washing the bad stuff away, but it can make you feel like you're chopping onions in a cry-fest!

FUN FACT: There's a trick to avoid the tears! You can try chilling the onion before cutting it or cutting it under running water. Both methods help reduce the amount of tear-inducing gas that gets released into the air, so you can slice without the waterworks.

So, onions aren't out to make you cry — they're just defending themselves with a little chemical reaction that sends your tear ducts into overdrive!

HOW OLD IS THE OLDEST LIVING TREE?

The oldest known living tree is an incredible over *5,000 years old!* This ancient tree, named *Methuselah*, is a bristlecone pine found in California's White Mountains. It's been standing tall since long before the pyramids were even built, making it one of the most ancient living organisms on Earth!

But how do people figure out a tree's age? Scientists use a method called tree-ring dating or *dendrochronology.* Every year, a tree grows a new ring inside its trunk. In good years, when there's plenty of water and sunlight, the ring is wider. In harsher years, it's narrower. By counting these rings, scientists can estimate the tree's age. For really ancient trees like Methuselah, they use a special tool called a borer to remove a small sample from the tree's trunk without harming it, so they can count the rings without cutting it down.

Fun fact: Methuselah's exact location is kept top-secret to protect it from being damaged by visitors. And while Methuselah is the oldest living non-clonal tree, there's an even older clonal tree called Old Tjikko in Sweden, which is over 9,500 years old. Its root system is ancient, but the visible part of the tree is much younger!

These ancient trees are living time capsules, silently witnessing thousands of years of history while standing strong!

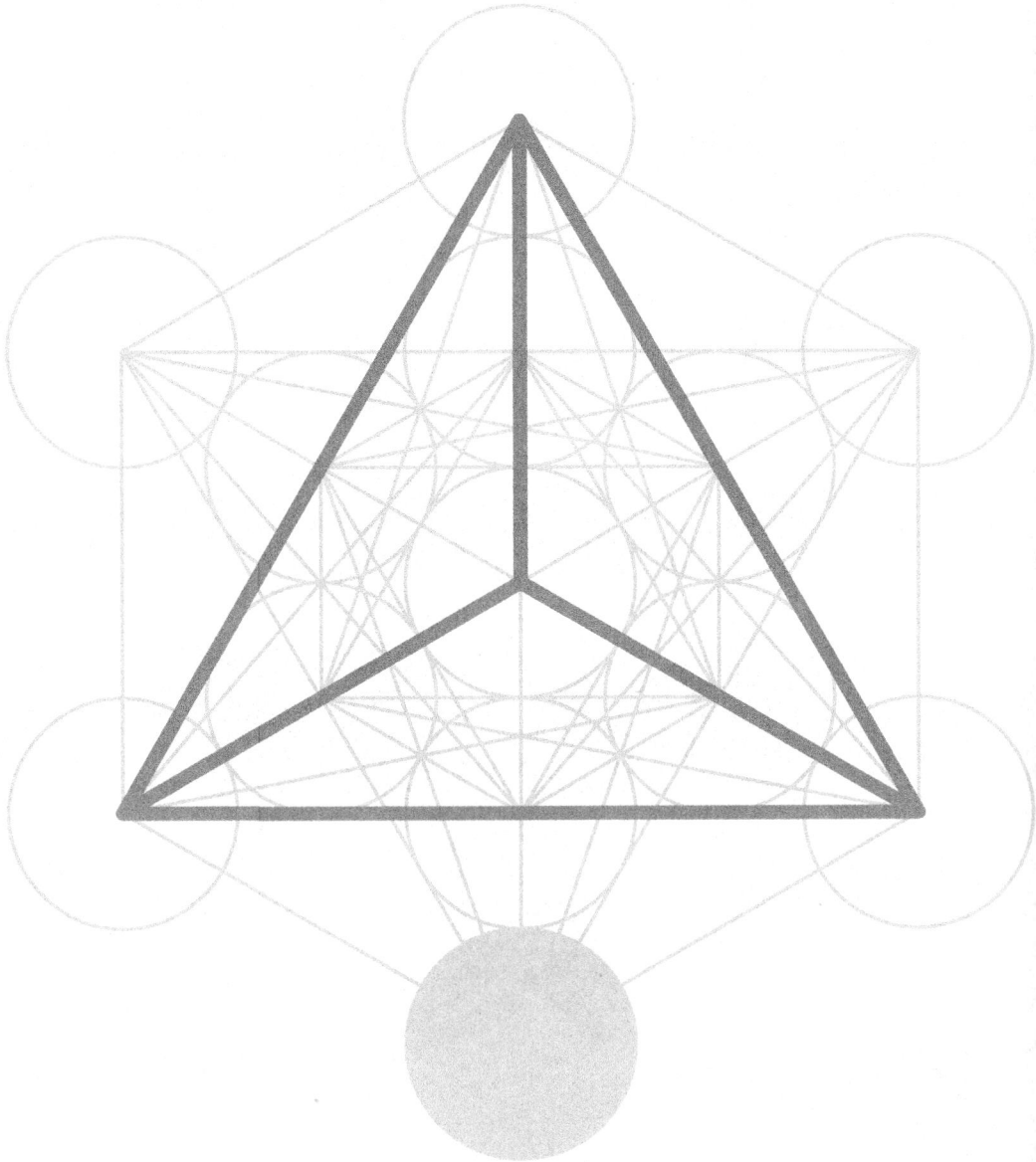

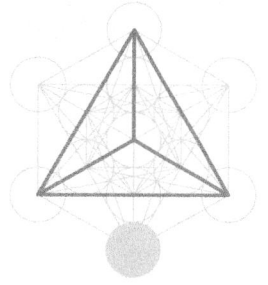

HISTORICAL GENIUSES

WHO WAS LEONARDO DA VINCI, AND WHY WAS HE A GENIUS?

Leonardo da Vinci was like the OG multitasker — *the ultimate Renaissance man!* Born in 1452, this dude didn't just stick to one thing. He was a next-level artist, inventor, scientist, and engineer all rolled into one. His curiosity was off the charts, and he wanted to know how literally everything worked. That's what made him such a genius!

As an artist, he's famous for painting the *Mona Lisa* (yep, the most famous painting ever) and The Last Supper. He was all about capturing real emotions, and his attention to detail was wild. He was also low-key obsessed with human anatomy, so he studied the body to make sure everything in his art looked super realistic.

But here's where it gets even cooler — Leonardo wasn't just about art. He filled his notebooks with designs for all kinds of crazy inventions, like *flying machines, robots*, and even *scuba gear!* He dreamed up things that didn't even exist yet, and some of his ideas weren't built until hundreds of years later. Dude was way ahead of his time.

Leonardo was also a total science nerd. He sketched detailed drawings of everything from muscles to machines. He studied how birds fly and even dissected human bodies to understand how they worked. His notebooks were packed with all this info, and some of his discoveries laid the groundwork for stuff we use today.

What made him a genius? He could mix art and science like nobody else. He didn't just paint pretty pictures; he used science to make them more real.

And he didn't just design cool inventions — he studied nature and used that knowledge to fuel his ideas.

Fun fact: Leonardo wrote a lot of his notes in "mirror writing" — backward! We're still not sure why he did it. Some say he was trying to keep his ideas secret, others think it was just easier for him because he was left-handed. Either way, it's just another reason why he was one of a kind!

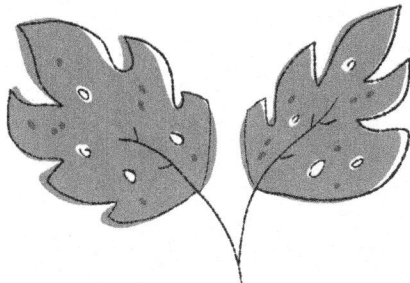

WHO IS **ALBERT EINSTEIN,** AND WHY IS HE CONSIDERED ONE OF THE SMARTEST PEOPLE EVER?

Albert Einstein was basically *the king of brainpower*! Born in 1879, he changed the way we understand the universe and became a legend in the world of science. You've probably heard his name linked to the word "genius," and for good reason — his ideas were so wild, they completely shook up what scientists thought they knew.

Einstein is most famous for his *theory of relativity.* Ever heard of *E=mc²*? That's him! It's one of the most famous equations in the world, and it basically says that energy and matter are two sides of the same coin. This idea helped explain things like how stars work and even how nuclear energy is possible. His theory also showed that time and space are connected, which blew people's minds. Time doesn't tick the same everywhere in the universe — it can actually slow down or speed up depending on how fast you're moving or how close you are to something super massive like a black hole!

$$E = MC^2$$

What makes Einstein a genius isn't just his smarts — it's how he thought differently. He questioned everything and used thought experiments to figure stuff out, imagining himself riding on beams of light or floating in space. His imagination was next-level, and he used it to solve problems no one else could.

Even though his theories were pretty hard for most people to understand at first, Einstein helped change the entire field of physics. His ideas laid the foundation for modern technology, like GPS, which wouldn't work without his discoveries about how time and space behave.

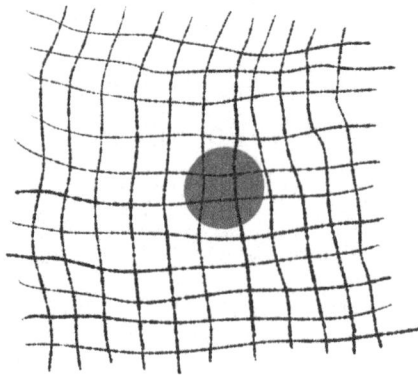

Fun fact: When Einstein was a kid, his teachers didn't think he was very smart! He was slow to start talking, and he didn't always do well in school. But he ended up proving that thinking outside the box is what makes a true genius. He's now one of the most famous scientists ever!

WHO IS ADA LOVELACE, AND WHY IS SHE CALLED THE FIRST COMPUTER PROGRAMMER?

Ada Lovelace was basically the original tech queen — born in 1815, she's known as the world's *first computer programmer*, even though computers didn't exist yet! How's that possible? Well, she was a visionary who saw the potential of machines way before anyone else did.

Ada worked with a mathematician named *Charles Babbage*, who designed an early machine called *the Analytical Engine*, which was like the great-great-grandparent of modern computers. While Babbage focused on building it, Ada realized something no one else did — this machine could do more than just crunch numbers. She thought it could follow instructions to perform more complex tasks, like writing music or solving puzzles.

Her real genius moment came when she wrote what's considered the first algorithm — basically, a set of instructions for the Analytical Engine to follow. That's why she's called the first computer programmer! Ada's ideas were way ahead of her time, and it wasn't until over 100 years later that computers became advanced enough to use programs like the one she imagined.

Even though Ada was a tech genius, she was also super creative. She loved poetry, and she believed that imagination and logic went hand-in-hand. She saw computers not just as tools for math, but as machines that could one day do anything – kind of like what our smartphones and laptops do today!

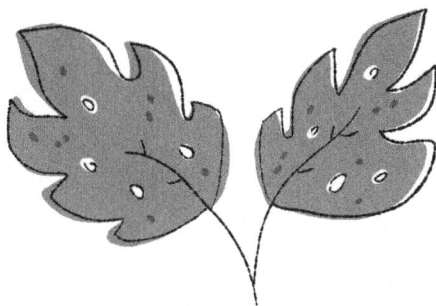

WHO WAS MARIE CURIE, AND HOW DID SHE CHANGE SCIENCE FOREVER?

Marie Curie was a trailblazing scientist who changed the world with her groundbreaking discoveries in radioactivity. Born in 1867 in Poland, she was the first woman to win *a Nobel Prize* — and not just one, but two! She was also the first person ever to win Nobel Prizes in two different sciences: Physics and Chemistry.

Marie Curie and her husband, Pierre Curie, discovered two new elements: *polonium* and *radium*, both of which are radioactive. But Marie did more than just discover these elements — she figured out how radioactivity worked, which opened the door to all sorts of new technologies, like *X-rays*. In fact, during World War I, she helped equip ambulances with X-ray machines to help doctors see broken bones on the battlefield.

Her work wasn't just important — it was game-changing. She laid the foundation for advances in nuclear energy and cancer treatment, and her research is still shaping science today. Despite facing a lot of challenges, like being a woman in science during a time when women were often not taken seriously, Marie pushed through and made some of the most important discoveries in history.

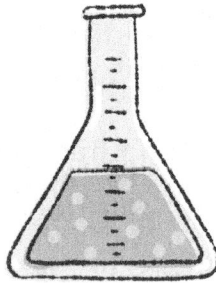

Fun fact: Marie Curie's notebooks are still so radioactive that they're stored in special lead boxes! Even though she didn't know how dangerous radiation could be, she was fearless in her research, and her work forever changed how we understand the world.

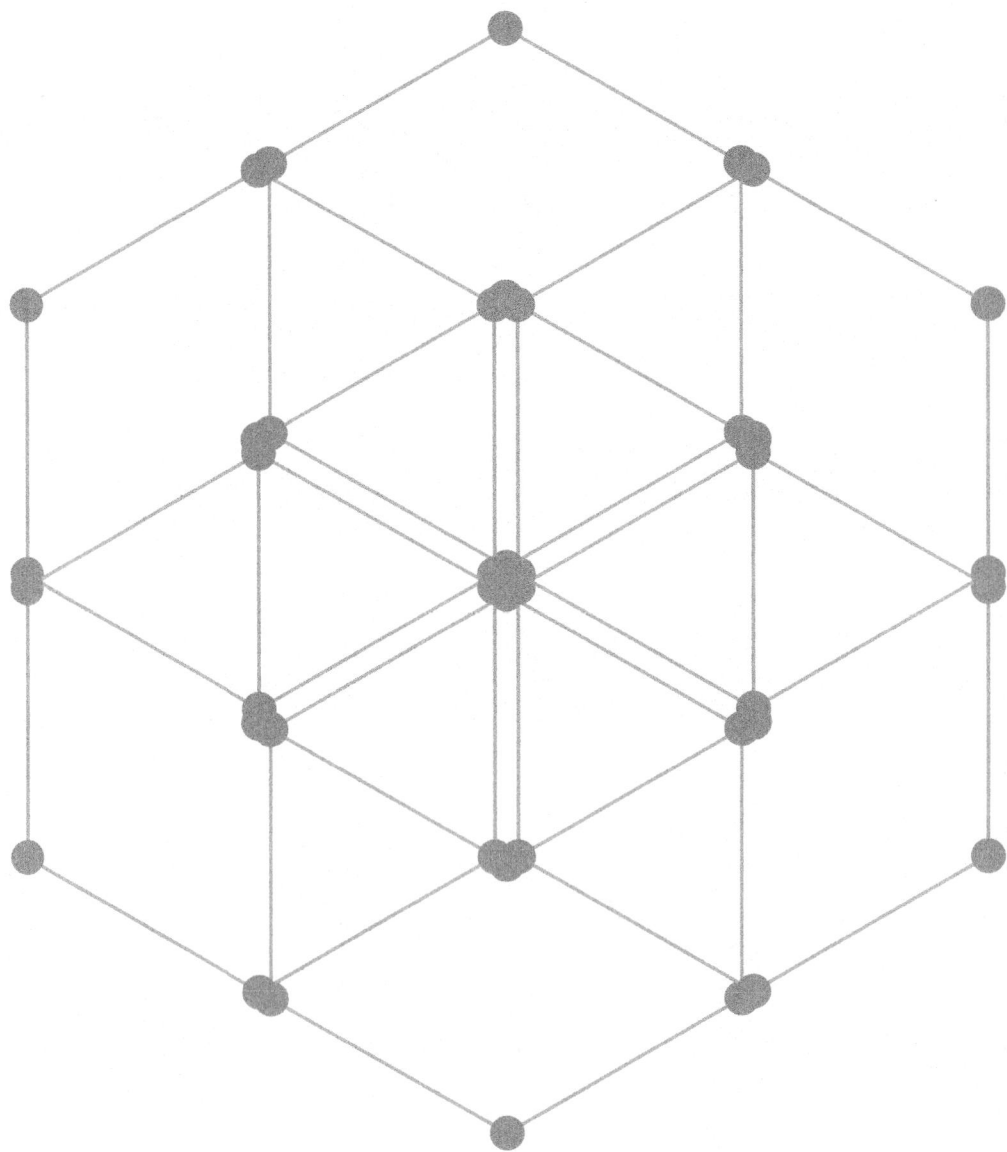

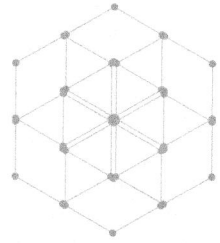

MIND-BLOWING MYSTERIES OF THE WORLD

The questions that are yet to be solved!

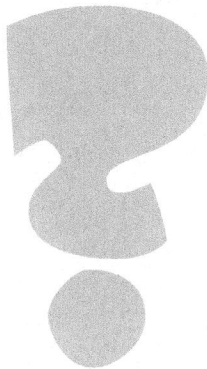

WHO BUILT STONEHENGE, AND WHY?

Stonehenge is one of the greatest mysteries in the world! This massive circle of stones in England has been standing for over *4,000 years,* but the big question is — who built it and why? Archaeologists believe it was constructed by ancient peoples, possibly *the Neolithic or Bronze Age* civilizations, but no one knows for sure.

The stones used to build Stonehenge are massive, and some of them were transported from over *150 miles away!* How these ancient builders managed to move such huge stones without modern technology is still a head-scratcher. Some theories suggest they used logs, ropes, or even boats to get the stones into place.

As for why it was built, there are plenty of theories. Some believe Stonehenge was a temple for worship, others think it was an astronomical calendar used to track the movements of the Sun and Moon, especially during the

195

summer and winter solstices. Another idea is that it was a burial ground or a place of healing. Some even say aliens had something to do with it — though that's more of a fun myth than a fact!

While we might never know the full story behind Stonehenge, one thing's for sure — it's one of the most fascinating and mysterious monuments ever created!

Fun fact: During the summer solstice, the Sun rises perfectly in line with the stones at Stonehenge, which has led many to believe it was used to mark important astronomical events.

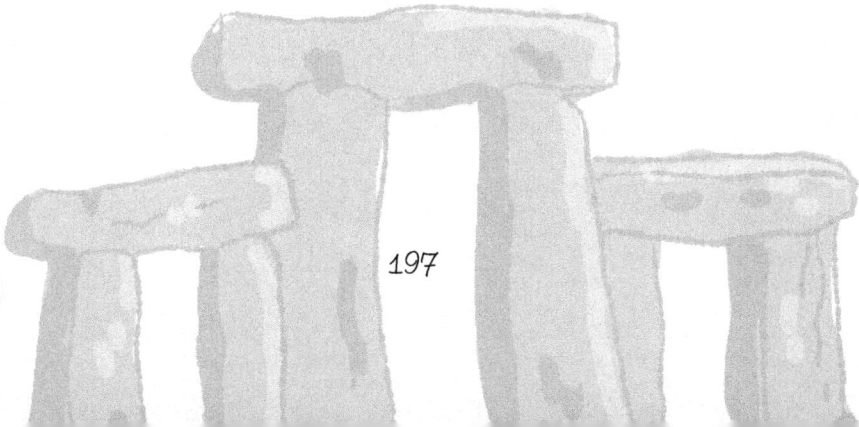

WHAT'S REALLY GOING ON IN THE BERMUDA TRIANGLE?

The Bermuda Triangle is one of the world's biggest mysteries, and it's known for causing some serious weirdness! This area, stretching between *Miami, Bermuda,* and *Puerto Rico,* has been linked to the mysterious disappearances of ships, planes, and even entire crews. But the real question is: what's going on there?

Over the years, people have come up with all kinds of theories to explain the strange events. Some believe there are supernatural forces at work, like aliens or underwater cities pulling ships and planes off course. Others suggest it could be magnetic anomalies that mess with navigational equipment, causing ships and planes to get lost.

Scientists, however, have looked for more down-to-earth explanations. One theory is that sudden, violent storms or rogue waves could explain the disappearances.

Another idea is that the area's strong currents and deep trenches create dangerous waters that can quickly swallow ships. Some researchers even think that methane gas bubbles rising from the ocean floor could cause vessels to lose buoyancy and sink without warning!

The truth is, there's no solid answer yet, and many of the disappearances remain unsolved. Whether it's natural phenomena, magnetic fields, or something we haven't discovered yet, the Bermuda Triangle continues to be a place that stirs up curiosity – and a little bit of fear!

Fun fact: Despite its spooky reputation, thousands of ships and planes pass through the Bermuda Triangle every year without any issues. Most scientists agree that the area is no more dangerous than any other part of the ocean, but the mystery still lingers!

WHAT'S AT THE BOTTOM OF THE OCEAN?

The deep ocean is like Earth's final frontier — a place so vast and unexplored that we've only scratched the surface of what's down there! In fact, over 80% of the ocean remains unexplored, which makes the question, *"What's at the bottom of the ocean?"* one of the greatest mysteries ever.

At the deepest part of the ocean, known as the Mariana Trench, the pressure is so intense that most life as we know it couldn't survive. But that hasn't stopped crazy creatures from thriving there! Scientists have discovered some wild species, like the anglerfish with its *glowing lure, giant squids,* and even *jellyfish* that look straight out of a sci-fi movie. These animals have adapted to the extreme darkness, freezing temperatures, and crushing pressure in ways that still blow scientists' minds.

Beyond the strange sea creatures, there could be underwater volcanoes, deep-sea vents, and even undiscovered ecosystems. Some believe there might even be hidden treasures or ancient shipwrecks lost to time. The ocean floor is also covered with unique geological features like underwater mountains, canyons, and ridges that we've barely begun to map.

But there's more than just natural wonders. Some scientists think that studying the bottom of the ocean could reveal clues about Earth's history, like how continents were formed or where life on Earth began. There's even a chance we could find new medicines from deep-sea organisms that could help cure diseases.

The truth is, we've explored more of outer space than we have of the deep ocean, and who knows what we'll find as technology allows us to go deeper. The bottom of the ocean remains one of Earth's most exciting, mysterious, and unexplored places!

Fun fact: The deepest part of the ocean, the Challenger Deep in the Mariana Trench, is nearly 36,000 feet deep — that's deeper than Mount Everest is tall! And yet, we've only visited it a handful of times, making it one of the most mysterious places on the planet.

TIME TO THINK LIKE A GENIUS!

Whoa, you made it to the end — and now you're packed with mind-blowing facts, wild ideas, and some epic genius-level knowledge! From the mysteries of space to the secrets behind nature's coolest tricks, you've just unlocked a treasure trove of answers to the questions that make the world so awesome.

But here's the thing: learning never really ends. Every question you ask opens the door to even more incredible discoveries, and the best part? You get to be the one to explore them. Whether you're dreaming of building the next big invention, solving nature's most puzzling mysteries, or even blasting off to Mars one day, your curiosity is the ultimate superpower.

So what's next? Keep asking questions. Keep exploring the world around you. And don't be afraid to think big—just like the geniuses you've learned about in this book. Who knows, one day, it might be your ideas that change the game and inspire the world!

Until then, stay curious, keep thinking like a genius, and remember: the adventure never stops when your brain's always on!

Now go out there and blow some minds!

GLOSSARY

Artificial Intelligence (AI)

A type of technology that allows machines, like robots and computers, to learn from experience and solve problems—just like humans! AI helps machines get smarter the more they practice.

Bioluminescence

A natural process where living things, like fireflies or jellyfish, create and give off light. It's kind of like their built-in glow stick!

Black Hole

A super powerful space object with such strong gravity that not even light can escape it! They form when giant stars collapse at the end of their lives.

Event Horizon

The "point of no return" around a black hole. Once something crosses it, it gets pulled into the black hole forever!

Filament

A super thin wire inside a light bulb that glows when electricity passes through it, creating light.

Gravity

An invisible force that pulls objects toward each other. Gravity is what keeps us on Earth and what makes things fall when you drop them.

Hexagon

A shape with six sides. Bees use hexagons to build their hives because it's strong and efficient, taking up the least space while storing the most honey.

Luciferin

A special chemical found in animals like fireflies that helps them produce light through a chemical reaction.

Machine Learning

A part of Artificial Intelligence (AI) where machines

(like robots) can learn from experience and improve over time without needing to be reprogrammed.

Neural Network

A computer system designed to work like the human brain. It helps machines, like robots, recognize patterns and make decisions, just like we do when we learn something new.

Nuclear Fusion

A process that happens inside stars (like the Sun) where hydrogen atoms smash together to form helium, releasing a huge amount of energy in the form of light and heat.

Photosynthesis

The process plants use to turn sunlight into food. They take in sunlight, water, and carbon dioxide, and make energy to grow.

Protoplanetary Disk

A huge, spinning disk of gas and dust that forms around a young star. Over time, bits of the disk stick together to form planets, moons, and other space objects.

Radioactivity

The process where certain elements give off energy as they break down. This is what makes radium and polonium, two elements discovered by Marie Curie, glow and give off radiation.

Thrust

The force that pushes an object forward, like how an airplane's engines help it move through the air.

Vacuum

A space that has no air or matter in it. Outer space is a vacuum, which is why astronauts need spacesuits to protect them since there's no air to breathe!

Algorithm

A set of instructions a computer or robot follows to solve a problem or complete a task, kind of like a recipe in a cookbook.

Singularity

The center of a black hole where all its mass is squished into a tiny space. It's the point where gravity is at its strongest.

Dendrochronology

The science of figuring out how old trees are by studying their rings. Each ring represents one year of growth!

LiDAR

A technology that uses lasers to measure distances and map out environments. Self-driving cars use LiDAR to "see" what's around them.

BACK BLURB

Ready to dive into a world where facts get fun, and curiosity takes over? *Think Like a Genius* is your all-access pass to mind-boggling answers for all those questions you've always wondered about — and a few you haven't even thought of yet! From how planes stay in the sky to what would happen if you fell into a black hole (yep, it's wild), this book's packed with epic explanations, weird-but-true facts, and the coolest science, nature, and space mysteries you can imagine.

Why don't we feel the Earth zooming through space? How do robots think? What makes bees obsessed with hexagons? Grab your snacks and thinking cap, because we're about to break down everything from 3D printers to how video games get made. And by the end, you'll be flexing your genius-level knowledge like a total brainiac!

So, what are you waiting for? Unlock the ultimate guide to curious questions and discover the seriously cool stuff that's happening all around you. Time to Think Like a Genius!

Inside, you'll explore:

- The secret behind why the Earth doesn't feel like it's spinning—when it's moving at 1,000 mph!

- How 3D printers work and the amazing things they can create (including pizza!)

- What would actually happen if you fell into a black hole (spoiler: it's wild!)

- How bees use hexagons to build perfect, space-saving hives

- The truth behind self-driving cars and how they know where to go

- Why robots are getting smarter every day — thanks to Artificial Intelligence (AI)

Ready for answers that'll blow your mind? Let's go!

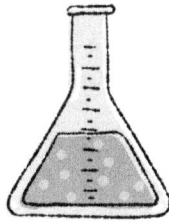

Printed in Dunstable, United Kingdom